Why Ask Why? WHEN YOU SAY WE'RE STUPID ANYWAY

Why Ask Why? WHEN YOU SAY WE'RE STUPID ANYWAY

WHEN YOU'RE TRYING TO FIGURE OUT WHY YOU KEEP CHOOSING THE WRONG COMPANION.

JAWORSKI D. COFFEY

Why Ask Why?: When You Say We're Stupid Anyway
Copyright © 2022 by Jaworski D. Coffey. All rights reserved.

No part of this publication may be reproduced, stored in a retrieval system or transmitted in any way by any means, electronic, mechanical, photocopy, recording or otherwise without the prior permission of the author except as provided by USA copyright law.

The opinions expressed by the author are not necessarily those of URLink Print and Media.

1603 Capitol Ave., Suite 310 Cheyenne, Wyoming USA 82001
1-888-980-6523 | admin@urlinkpublishing.com

URLink Print and Media is committed to excellence in the publishing industry.

Book design copyright © 2022 by URLink Print and Media. All rights reserved.

Published in the United States of America

Library of Congress Control Number: 2022907126
ISBN 978-1-68486-171-2 (Paperback)
ISBN 978-1-68486-172-9 (Digital)

04.04.22

CONTENTS

Author's Thoughts 7

Knowing Who You Are Dealing With 19

The Crazy Guy 23

Momma's Boy 29

The Drama King 33

The Jealous Guy 37

The Focused Guy 41

The Stand-Up Guy 45

Liar, Liar 49

The Playboy 51

Mr. Ohh Wee 53

Mr. Unavailable 55

The Leach 59

Trust 61

Cheating 77

Communication 91

Placement 105

Break Ups 117

Compatibility 131

Sex 145

Love, Happiness, and Peace of Mind 153

What Women Want to Know 161

Acknowledgments 177

AUTHOR'S THOUGHTS

In the beginning and the end of everything of our lives we say we know what we want, but do we truly know. We all believe we know what it is we want in and out of life but for the most part, when it comes to the relationship aspect of our lives, sometimes we really don't know. From my travels, I have found this to be true on a number of occasions and in many different situations. Let's just say if you took out the time and made a list of the things in your life that makes you smile, the list would be a pretty long list for some or a very simple one for others. But what most of us don't understand is this list I speak of is an ever-changing list and from time to time as we grow into who we are trying to become, this list changes as we change or, as I like to say, we evolve. Because what made you a little happy yesterday, may not be as enlightening to us today.

It's not that we don't know what it is we want. It's just as we evolve into the human beings we are becoming our wants, needs, and desires change as the weather changes. A salad from your favorite restaurant satisfied your hunger yesterday but you have a different taste bud working on your hunger today. It's not that it won't taste as good but could you imagine eating the same thing every day. Where is the fun in that? The same way we treat our hunger, we treat our lives. This works the same for our relationships as it does for everything else in our lives. This means our clothes, the way we wear our hair, the way we exercise, or even the products we use to clean our bodies. It seems as though everything we deal with just changes. We may love the ride of the new car we bought a year ago gives us, but a couple of years or so passes by and we see something that is just a little more appealing to us. We want it and we get it to see if it is as we think it is.

Don't think there is anything wrong with you, like you have some type of disorder or phobia. Our desires change with time and with us being the people we are, we simply like what we like. With time, all things change. The summers get a little bit hotter and the winters get a little colder. For you to want something better is not a problem but to go into something without any knowledge of what is to come is a problem. Sometimes it is a good idea to think things through with a great deal of passiveness because our desires can and sometimes will outweigh our needs and our eyes blind our reason from rational thinking.

The hard part about all of this is when our desires change, we have a tendency not to know it and this is what causes more problems in relationships simply because our minds and our hearts aren't on the same page of thinking any more. This causes a number of problems within the sanctity of a relationship because with change come questions and with questions there should come answers. Sometimes the right answers aren't always given or answers are just not given at all.

Having no answers always presents a major problem because "I don't know" is never a good answer to any question in the heat of the moment of a kindled discussion with the one you love or the one you say you love.

Just because the understanding of an action its self is not there, there is a reason for every action taken no matter how perplexing or how juvenile it is. There is always an answer. Although at the time we may not know or don't want to say but there has to be an answer for everything we decide to do in our daily lives. Some things we don't have answers for simply because there is an unknown and unseen being that takes part in our lives.

Other than that we must put forward all efforts to present a better way of saying the things we really mean and not just reacting off our impulses and our emotions. Even though we are our own beings and don't owe an explanation to anyone about the things we do, just remember this: The unspoken word always hurt more than any spoken insult could. Because when you're not sure about the person you're with and how they are thinking, the door of wondering is opened and for most of us when that door is left open our mind's have a tendency to think the absolute worst.

This is the point when you think things can't get any worse with enough time and effort left out of the relationship things can and will get even worse, especially when we are left to let our imaginations go and don't have any restrictions. We can go as long as we are left out there by ourselves without a proper explanation. When a question of any kind is not properly answered, this causes uncertainty and like the G.I. Joe slogan says, "Knowing is half the battle." In whatever it is we do, understanding is the best thing in the world. If we have knowledge about the most important things in our lives and in our minds, this helps us to truly be peaceful within our hearts and our minds about the decisions we make. So if you cannot think of a good reason for whatever it is you have done at that point and time, do yourself and the person you are with a huge favor. Let the other party know it is not a good time to talk and you will discuss it later to give yourself some time to try and figure things out. Just don't let later become a thing of the past because if you wait too long to give an explanation of the actions you've taken, you will eventually find yourself by yourself and loneliness is one of the worst feelings any person can ever feel.

Most people don't understand the stages that have to be followed as time progresses in the relationship. As the individual matures and grows, the relationship itself should progress as well. The conventional meet a girl, date a girl, marry a girl, and have children, while building a foundation is a nice concept but it seems to be a thing of the past. That concept has worked for the older generations whom have maintained the focus of how their parents did it and how they were told how it was supposed to go. It just doesn't happen like that as much as it used to in this day and age.

In this era, there are so many of us trying to grow into successful and wholesome individuals in life that there seems to be no more room for anything else other than just trying to make a living and make a way for ourselves. The woman is a more independent individual in this day and time simply because of the growth of the single parent households and the struggles of life have gotten a little more difficult to deal with. It seems kind of selfish but that's just how it is now, where job and career comes before family and it is fairly simple because you need the job to maintain the house the family lives in. That's not by choice but how society has made it. Having good career, a peaceful state of mind, having a dream of being successful, and having nice things are great ideas but this leaves us to neglect some of the more important elements in our lives. For most of us when our relationships are disrupted for any reason, it causes unnecessary heartache and stress that can disrupt our daily lives.

For me this is an instructional guide to help those who really can't understand why we as men do some of the unbelievable things we do and for those who really are in need of some factual answers. There isn't much you as women can do. You can try and figure things out on your own but we all need a little help with understanding some of the wonders in life. Even some of you men can learn something about yourselves in reading this.

Ladies I will use this as an example. When your man has done something or said something you just can't believe and for you, his answers are just not good enough and in the back of your mind you are wondering, what in the hell he was thinking when he did what he did. These are times when, "I don't know" or "you know why" just aren't good enough answers for the circumstances at hand. You know when your guy goes out and stays out into the wee hours of the morning and can't give you a suitable reason for doing so.

Or how about this one, when you catch your man cheating, he lies and doesn't give you a straight answer, and dodges you or tries to avoid the conversation at all costs. These are just a few of reasons why I wrote this guide of understanding. This for me is a comprehensive state of mind I wish to share with the misguided minds out there. For the ones out there who actually wants answers to situations they can't figure out themselves. All I ask of you is to be a little open-minded and a tad bit patient with me so I can try to help the relationships of your life get a little better, by something as simple as the type of men you allow into your lives.

Having an open-mind to the ideas expressed in this writing should be simple because some of the things you will read don't necessarily define your entire situation but it will touch you like no other has. I ask for a small amount of patience so you will not rush it because the information is coming and it will be some of the best information you have ever read.

I am not claiming to be the best writer ever born, or a relationship guru but I am claiming to be a man who has been through my share of ups and downs in my life and in my relationships. I have seen mostly good times which have made me smile from time to time and I have been through some of the worst relationship changes that have ever been heard of. Whether they affected me directly or indirectly. I look at myself as the big brother of the house that always get asked the tough questions from my younger siblings about the trials and tribulations of my life and I answer with complete honesty because I don't want to see them go through what I have gone through and I don't want them to have to feel the pains I have had to endure.

I don't claim to have a PhD in psychology or claim to be a shrink or anything of that nature, but I do have a Personal but Honest and Disciplined way of looking and going about certain aspects of life that have gotten me to this point. I am just a person with a lot on my mind and need to get some of this goodness off of my shoulders and share it with the people who can use it to grow from. In this little simple life I have lived, I have helped a number of people who I consider friends with some of the problems in their relationships with something as simple as keeping an open ear, evaluating the problem, and giving them an honest answer whether they liked the answers or not.

So hopefully your reading of this will somehow help you out with the life you are living and help put a positive spin on your existing relationship or your future one or ones to come. We all need some type of help to get to where we want to go in life and the easier our lives can be the less stressful it will be. For you all that gain something from this, I will like to say I do truly apologize for the wait because I was supposed to have already had this writing done years ago but I have grown to understand we all move at God's speed. Well I guess some things in life are worth waiting for and I hope you have as much fun reading this as I had writing it because this has been a journey for me to have made it this far.

Some of our secrets will be released with this writing but gentlemen it is for the best. It isn't anything that hasn't already been told, I am just going to go deeper than most have gone and just simplify men for men because someone has to put forth the effort to help our women understand us. If they have a better understanding of who we are as men this will make different aspects of our lives a little easier to deal with. Could you imagine a narrated story of your lives which gives a more submerged perception of the every day trials we go through in dealing with our women? A number of you will learn a little something about yourself in your readings and some of you may not like some of the things that may come out but you will be fine.

In writing this I have learned a lot more about myself because even though I have taken some of the things others have gone through and put them into my own words. Some of the experiences from my life are also included in this. There were a few things deep within me that were brought out I feel will help make me to be a better man for the one I am with. In opening my mind and my heart to you I feel like I have become a better me.

Ask yourself this, have you ever been some where and done something you really couldn't explain why you did it? I have been there too and to just be truthful about it, the only reason why I didn't have an answer is simply because I didn't think everything through and that is why I ended up like

I did. If we actually took the time to things things through before we did them, things will have never turned out the way they did. Then again we may not have done it all. Its sad to say but we all have to learn, some the hard way. All that is needed is to take a deep breath and take four to seven seconds to think about the matter at hand and this will help to keep us out of some of the troubles that can come up in your life.

If you have ever gone against the same moral fiber that makes you the person you are and you can't figure out why, this is the guide to help you and your life. Sometimes the answers don't form in our membrane because we are always looking for excuses or faults in someone else to justify what it is we have done and our clouded judgments are the reasons why we had to deal with the situations we have ended up in. For the most part, we sometimes need an outside source to help us understand our problems because the source doesn't have any reason to be bias and this way they can give you the truth. Even though it may be a little raw, but it is what they have observed about the matter. This book is just that, a little help for the common problems we face on a daily basis no matter how simple the problems we deal with in our relationships.

As I am growing into the man I am to become my Father has also given me a few special gifts I cherish with all of my being and they are the main focus for this writing. At first, this was an idea of a future father to write a list of situations down which my daughters may encounter with the men in their lives. By me being the man I am and I have gone through some of the same issues they will encounter in their future. I had to make sure I have a vast knowledge about these things so if they did feel comfortable enough to come to me wanting answers, I would be able to answer their questions without hesitation. In writing this I was told there were a lot of women out there in this world who need this information and need it now. My daughters are young and it will be a number of years that are going to pass before either one of them will have any questions of this magnitude or before I will have these types conversation with them. That's why I took the time to write this because I felt if I didn't lift a finger to help someone who really needed it and I didn't do anything to help, I would be less than I say I am as a man. I know when you are dealing with human beings mistakes are possible and are probable because we all make mistakes. Sometimes it is an outside influence that interferes in the matters of our lives but we have to grow up and deal with them and stop making excuses for the mistakes we make along the way.

Since the influence starts early, this is for you to better understand the male race and why we do as we do. This is for all the Angels, the Kims, the Christines but no matter your name and what it is you are going through, if I can help any of you I will. Even though I may not be able to have direct contact with you, this writing is me reaching out to you no matter what you have gone through. This is for those that have gone throughout life without the appropriate guidance that I plan to give my angels and no matter what your name is or your occupation, this is for you.

Sometimes it is difficult to figure out why things happen. But it is more perplexing to and figure out, "why things keep happening" to you in your relationship and this is not to try and shift the blame on one person because it's not just a one person in a relationship. But if you have an understanding of why these mistakes are happening, you can do better because you can figure out "Why" a lot easier and a lot faster. Hopefully this will help you to move on forward with your lives and help you to be able to deal with the issues you may face so enjoy and again I say thank you.

KNOWING WHO YOU ARE DEALING WITH

Before I get started, let me inform you of a few things that will help you to identify with the person whom you are calling your man, your bae, your love, or whatever the adjective you use to describe him. For starters allow me to say this, all men are not the same and for you to appreciate your man for what he is and what he has to offer to the relationship. First you have to try to realize what it is that makes him tick or what kind of guy he is. For this reason and this reason alone is why you can't walk into all relationships with the same attitude because most men have some of the same characteristics but each and every one of them are different in their own little way because they have their own ways of dealing with the situations in their lives. Each and every man you run across is going to have something different to offer it's just you have to be able to determine exactly what that is and sometimes finding out becomes the hard part because it seems to take too long and your patience may wear a little thin.

When I say, "offer" it's not just a financial thing. There are many things a man has to offer in a relationship like good friendship, moral support, spiritual guidance, or just being able to be the best man he could be in the bed. Men have different motivational factors in life that drive them down the roads they are traveling and, believe it or not, its not up to you to figure out what road it is. What hinders this process is when a man hasn't learned to open up and that's where some of the problems comes in. The problem is not you, but you have to understand for most men it is so hard to open up to anyone because sometimes communication problems seem to be a tough task for most men. The best thing you can do is be patient because depending on the level of comprehension the man has, it may take a while. First you need to find what it is you need to do to make yourself happy. Do what you can to make him happy as well just remember, sometimes you can't satisfy everyone but learn to make yourself happy and the rest will follow. As your man gets comfortable with you, a line of communication will get turned on with unlimited talk and nation-wide usage will be in full affect.

Most women don't understand they actually have the power to dictate all aspects of their relationship and even though you may want a man to lead you, sometimes you have to take the initiative to be the leader from time to time in order to get some balance in the relationship. Sometimes you ladies have to put in your heads and constantly remind yourselves that no matter how the relationship goes and grows, it is determined by what type of woman you are and what it is you want out of the relationship. The key is knowing exactly when to take the driver's seat and drive the relationship and when to take the passenger's seat and kick your feet up. You also have to be able to see things in a different manner because if there is an aspect of a man you "desire" and this man is not giving it to you, that may be because he doesn't have the qualities you are looking for. Or he may not desire to be that guy for you.

With the men you will come to meet in your life, remember all men are not to be labeled as one particular type and they may be a number of different types combined. He just favors one type stronger than others. Just like the different phases women go through men go through some of them as well. When men go through their phases it is something special to see. So pay attention because this will be a learning experience like no other, when a boy grows into a man. It's just one thing to remember if you're not paying enough attention to what is going on you will miss out on the signs that will save you a lot of heartache and pain because knowing what to look for can make the world seem like a much sweeter place. Plus the relationships go so much more smoother when you have an idea of what type of man you are trying to pair yourself off with.

THE CRAZY GUY

It can be difficult in determining what type of man you are dealing with; but for this reason I will make things a little easier for you. Since the rate on domestic crime is shooting through the roof at an alarming rate, I think the psychopathic, physical abuser, or the "he only hits me because he loves me" man should be the first on my list. This man may have come across as a good, trustworthy, and a wholesome guy at first but he will make a fool of you if you're not paying him the attention he thinks he deserves. This is one of the men who lives and thrives for the heartaches and physical pains of the drama that come in life. He will give you a number of signs to show you he has some type of problem but you will over look it because of love or whatever the reason may be.

Sometimes you may think you are in love and he cares for you and this may be true, but no one needs a man to be madly in love with them. If you have had to question something he has done like popped up at your house without calling, that is something you should watch because no matter what he tells you he was coming by looking to find something. To put it in terms you may understand if he shows you any sign of being crazy, it is a good chance he is and you are playing a very dangerous game with a ticking time bomb.

This kind is the worst of the worst just because there is nothing he won't do to get his point across. The so called "Crazy Guy" is the kind you do your best to stay away from at all costs. If for no other reason than your own safety, because at any time he could snap out and he will hurt you.

In the beginning, things may seem to be going fine but what you don't know is in a little time that ugly dragon rears it's head and will attempt to show his face and will eventually spits out it's hot flame. If you have ever been burned, you know how it hurts. This is the time you should take everything you have, pack it up, and leave. However some women will give him the benefit of doubt and allow him to figure out things to blame it on. His stressful job, his battered past, or him just having a bad day. There shouldn't be any excuse for him to do harm to you for any reason.

When it's all said and done there is no good reason for a man to abuse a woman. Whether it is mentally or physically, the sooner you realize it the better off you will be without him. After he hits you the first time, what will you say from there? Or will you just continue to come up with excuses for his behavior, or keep covering up his problems and your fears with makeup? The harming of another human being in the rights of protecting yourself is called self-defense but that's not what I am speaking of. What I am speaking of is simply, flat-out abuse.

This is the point of the relationship where he starts to declare his dominance over you because if he assaulted you in any way, either physically or verbally, it is time to start distancing yourself from him and, if you can, get as far away as you can to save yourself. Especially if there aren't any children involved in the relationship you should be able to leave when you want. If there is a child or children in the relationship, you have to put their needs and safety first. I am not saying he will hurt the children but you have to realize what you go through they go through too and the pains you feel hurt them too. The last thing you want is for your son to grow up thinking it is okay to harm a woman or your daughter growing up thinking a man doesn't love her unless he abuses her. The crazy one will eventually hurt you or someone around you with absolutely no remorse for his actions.

No matter how good you figure things have been in the past they are about to get a lot worse. It would seem as though you are with a totally different person. The man you fell in love with, the person you are accustomed to dealing with, will look the same but he will not be the same person. The happiness you thought you had in the beginning is about to turn into some of the worst pain you have ever felt in your life. The same man who used to bring some of the most beautiful smiles to your face will start to bring some of the biggest tears you have ever felt fall from your eyes. Those tears of joy have now turned into tears of sorrow and pain. If it gets as bad as I have seen it get, those mighty and heavy tears turn into tears of absolute fear.

Those tears alone can be the worse to bear because they come with a heavy price tag. This price tag I speak of has cost so many beautiful women the beauty God has given them. Not only has it caused this beauty to get battered and bruised but for some it has cost them their lives. Not because it was something they did but something they didn't do. That was to pay attention to the things that were unfolding around them. I have this saying I use from time to time to let people know I am always watching and that is, "It doesn't cost you nothing to pay attention." And even though this statement may be somewhat true but not paying attention can cost you your life.

I know there are many of us who watch the news and other television shows that air how tragic a relationship can turn out. Some of those same movies you watch and get so much enjoyment out of are based on true stories. Someone actually went through the same scenario you have watched and someone actually felt those pains. Those domestic crimes I speak of are on the rise are getting a lot worse. There used to be a time when a man would open a door to allow a woman to walk in before him out of respect for that woman. Now a man puts his woman in front of him because he doesn't trust her so he keeps her in front of him so he can keep an eye on her.

This man will change everything you hold near and dear to you, he will change the moral fiber of everything you cherish. He will drag you, your name, your family, and all you know down with him if he is allowed to. Like I said before, in a relationship the woman has the power to dictate the direction of the relationship. So if you feel it is time to say it's over, you need to say it because the last thing we need is another one of our beautiful young women to die for something so carelessly as an act of rage that could have been prevented.

This guy may become possessive and this possessiveness may come with a little aggression and with this aggression may come with a little physical abuse. So the next time you meet a guy and he gives you any sign he may be crazy or just a little off his rocker, be sure to give it some thought before you give him your number, because the life you might be able to save may just be your own.

MOMMA'S BOY

We all have an idea of someone who fits into this group, you know the "Momma's Boy." The one you can't get to grow up, fly right, and move out from under his mother's wings. He is thirty-something and is still getting ordered around by his mother like he is still a young teenager. He has absolutely no backbone as a man should. No matter how long you have been together and what you two have gone through, he still treats you like a sister from time to time. No matter how much you want him to step up to the plate and be the man you want him to be, he still can't find the intestinal fortitude to pave his own way. He works and may make a pretty good penny and instead of doing the manly thing like taking it upon himself and paying the bills, his woman has to ask him to do so. His woman has to do this time and time again in order to keep the bills paid. She has to point him in the direction he needs to be going in and it is almost like raising another child. He does what it takes when he wants to get between your thighs though.

This type of gentleman will work your last nerve. If this is the guy you want to lead you in the proper manner as a man should, he will not be able to because he doesn't have those leadership qualities in him. As a grown woman you don't identify with him well because he is too immature with the mindset of a young boy. He has been sheltered most of his life. His mother has done mostly everything for him and since he has grown dependent on her, he has developed insecurities. This man has too many uncertainties in his life and in his world he will always second guess everything his woman does because of the ideas of a woman's worth was predetermined for him by his mother. And even though a mother's love is one of the greatest feelings on this earth, a mother has to know when to let go. But more important than that, a boy has to realize when to become a man, thus carry and uplift himself as a man. This is the greatest obstacle he will ever have to overcome because even though it is not a difficult task to grow up, it is a difficult task when you don't know when you are all grown up. The mistake most people make is to put an age limit on adulthood. When it is more so built in the mental development of a person. The mental state helps to determine if you are grown up or not.

The problem with the momma's boy, or the cry baby, is he doesn't know how to let go. Everything you do is going to be compared to mom and sometimes it will be done unconsciously simply since he has been doing it for so many years of his life. That's why when you ask about some of his earlier relationships there are too many discrepancies in the reasons why they broke up. He can come up with a hundred-thousand reasons why it was her fault and what she did that he didn't agree with but in the end he will not give you one single reason why or what he has done to drive her to do the things she has done. Take this for instance: you have cooked one of the best dinners you have ever put together. His favorite dish, a nice twelve-ounce steak is grilled and seasoned to perfection, the garlic mashed potatoes are buttered to a golden glow, and the salad with all of his favorite condiments is chilled to a juicy crisp and instead of him telling you how delicious the meal is he says, "My mother used to cook just like this *but...*" Oh my, could you envision putting your best effort forward to please this ungrateful, inconsiderate, selfish, retard and getting nothing but complaints in return?

This *but* causes a lot of controversy in his relationships simply because most women will not tolerate it for long and some women are so headstrong they will not tolerate it at all. Ladies this is not a phase he is going through. He has grown set in his ways. It is not possible to break him but who wants to try and raise an already grown man into something he should already be. It is hard enough raising children up to act the way you want them to act. Just think of it like this, he is already an adult physically but he has a child's mentality. Don't fret it's not just you, all of his relationships will suffer even the bond he has with his friends suffers because he is so soft and timid. So with him you have to be careful because if you are too aggressive with him, you will run him off because he has a small fear of aggressive women or should I say strong women. Losing him because he is not strong enough to be the man you want, may not be a bad thing because he may not be the one for you because of his timidness and uncertainties.

With this type of man, no matter what you do there is nothing you can do to change what he has become. He has to be willing to change himself. You can't change it because there is nothing like a mother's love and no matter what you do, it isn't ever good enough. In time he may show you he has improved a little but after a while he will always revert back to his old ways. What you have to understand is he may have come from a broken home and his mother is all he knows. Add in a couple of sisters and no man in the house. This is a recipe for this mentality.

A good idea for you to put in place is you have to know he is like he is and what you have to do is be the strength your relationship needs. This isn't something you as a woman should have to do but if you want for the relationship to work you may have to be the mother of the relationship. When you do this you have to continue to do so and you have to keep your foot on his throat in order to reassure yourself he will move and develop as you need him to. Even though you may not want to, you have to in order to keep your sanity. So if you want someone you have to hold his hand and walk with him throughout the relationship. This is your man.

THE DRAMA KING

Just as women have a drama queen we as men also have an annoying, complaining, misguided, misunderstood, and silly friend we call the "Drama King." This is the guy no one ever cares to be or be around, but he always finds his way to where everyone is and works everyone's last nerve. He is the guy that comes into the barbershop and it never fails, he picks up an argument with anyone who is foolish enough to hold a conversation with him. This guy's whole objective is to frustrate anyone and everyone he can in any way he can by any means necessary. The tough part about this is he really can't help it even if he wanted to. In his little mind he thinks he is actually doing a good job of fitting in and may feel everyone enjoys his company but most of the people he comes in contact with really hate the sound of his voice. It's like scratching your fingernails across a chalkboard and the only person who enjoys the sound is the person doing the scratching.

The trouble with him is he really and deeply hates himself and doesn't know it. All he knows is he is right about everything. Sports, politics, cars, or whatever the topic is, he has a degree in all fields. Not because he knows what he is talking about, he just likes the sound of his own voice and toots his own horn a little bit too much. It's annoying as hell but the beautiful thing is you don't have to stay and listen to the things he is saying. You can pardon yourself from the conversation and move on.

With him comes his attitude and him being so obnoxious that you can't stand to hear him speak and it is so hard to ignore because it is so annoying it eats at your skin like radiation poisoning. There are plenty of unwanted characteristics that don't need explaining, he just rubs people the wrong way with his need for attention. This is your Mr. Know-it-all. He has his opinions and no matter how right you are with your point of view he still doesn't get it. It's like he enjoys the conflict and does whatever it takes to make a point of winning the discussion. He never listens to absorb the information. He listens so he can try and contradict anything being said.

Ladies listen, this is the last guy that any man wants to see you with because when you are associated with him it really aggravates most gentlemen. It's not that they are jealous or they envy him or anything of that nature. He just aggravates most to the point that guys don't like him and since your with him you get funny looks. Its not you it's him because every where he goes trouble follows because he just loves the attention. People can't seem to have a good time when he is around.

To be honest, if there wasn't something he has, like money or something materialistic that appeals to you, you probably wouldn't be with him. It's really kind of funny because he doesn't mean any harm to anyone but he brings problems his own way with no knowledge that he is doing so. If you looked at it in a different perspective, it's really sad because he will go through his whole life being that guy and may not even know he is that guy.

The deal with the Drama King is he has to be right about everything. He is never wrong and only sees the wrong others do or say. No matter how hard you try to do any good by him, he makes it difficult to do so. You know this man, he has a little bit of an education, maybe a degree in agriculture but he knows more about politics than the actual politicians. It is really difficult to do something like get a word in while having a conversation or even be able to get your point across. In dealing with this man, you have to remember it is hard to get him to understand when he doesn't even understand himself as a person. Just keep an eye open for this type because even though someone who knows it all knows it is not a good idea to flaunt you know everything because it seems as though you are rubbing it in people's faces and it's just annoying and this action alone can cause a number of people to dislike him.

THE JEALOUS GUY

This is one of the last guys you want to meet anywhere depending on what it is you are looking for in a man. If you like your privacy this may not be the one for you. With this one you will *have* to be extremely careful because you don't know when he will snap and show you a lot of unruly things that will scare you. Don't take this warning lightly, because if you do, it can cost you dearly. This is one of the guys your mother warned you about and if you don't take her advise please listen to mine. The real deal with him starts with the thick layer of insecurity he has and it starts with him and it spreads onto others at an alarming rate. "Sometimes a hard head can make a soft ass," well that's what my grandmother used to say and she never lead me wrong.

This guy is a special case because with the addition of a number of other characteristics he can be the one that changes your outlook on men as you see them today. He is the one that goes through your purse. The one that goes through your phone and calls numbers back. All men have a little bit of jealousy in them, or should I say a little bit of curiosity, but this one takes it to another level like no other. Most guys may wonder if his woman is cheating on him but this guy devises a plan that puts an inquisitive man to shame. This guy has good potential to be the next stalker in your life and if he has shown you any parts of him being aggressive, this may be a monster in the making. With a combination of aggression and jealousy, this man can turn ugly really fast.

He has all kinds of issues that don't have anything to do with you, but since you are with him you find out about these issues the hard way. The one issue that will stick out far from all the rest is the issue he has with trust. This issue isn't the only one he has but it is the major issue he has. I say this simply because he may not ever allow himself to trust you. He puts unnecessary pressure on you to be what he would like for you to be but you can do all he wishes but it will never be enough because of the issues dealing with his insecurity.

I am sure if you have met or heard about this guy and some of the things he has done. This is the one who knows his woman's should be at home thirty minutes after she gets off work because he has timed the route and if she detours any, he will know. This guy would much rather have his wife at home, barefoot, and pregnant as often as he can so he can keep tabs on her. This guy tries to make sure his woman doesn't have much of a social life, and tries to control every aspect of her life. This is the guy that has the most beautiful specimen of a woman but he doesn't want her to keep herself up.

The insecurities he has makes him question any relationship you have with another man. Your relationship with coworkers, the activities you have with your boss or maybe this one, what's so funny? Why are you laughing at his joke so hard?

He doesn't like her to put on makeup to enhance her beauty, or even wear a nice dress that makes her feel a little sexy in her mind. He does everything he can to hold her down and keep her dependent on him. He doesn't understand when she puts on something nice it is not for someone else. She just likes to feel good about her outward appearance and just wants to have a feeling of self-beauty not to impress anyone but to satisfy her own inner-confidence.

THE FOCUSED GUY

This is the guy who is not really interested in the every day relationship. With this guy comes something most people are really not accustomed to dealing with which is his headstrong attitude and his pursuit of the finer things in life. He is physically and mentally locked in on that and that alone. There is nothing on his mind but what it is he desires and the objectives at hand. If he is in school, his mind is on his studies. If he is an athlete, he has no real time for a girlfriend on the campus because his mind is set on his grades or maybe making it to the next level of the sport he is playing. If he is in the work force, trying to make a good life for himself and is fixed on moving up the corporate ladder. He will not let anyone or anything gets in his way. Don't think it is you, just remember he is trying to make a way of for himself to have a better life than the one he is used to seeing and doesn't want to settle for less, like so many of us have done.

This is the guy of your dreams if and only if he has already found his way. If he hasn't figured out what it is he is going to do with the rest of his life, he has no place for you if you're looking for a long term commitment. To be honest, if he is still trying to find his way he will not have time for you. Because you will get in the way of his ambitions. This is not a bad thing for him but for you he will be a good friend in the future, but for now he may be out of your reach. Not to the point where you can't touch him but as far as a relationship is concerned, he is not interested in that during his growing stage. A few one-night-standers or a half-way girlfriend and boyfriend relationship is what is most likely in this time. There is nothing serious. Maybe in a different day and time he will be the best person you have ever met but for now, you have to settle for the backseat.

On the other hand, if he has made it to the point where he is comfortable enough with having a regular significant other, he will be one of the best men you will ever come in contact with. Because now his focus has changed and at this time he may be focused on life and love and the same attention he put into his work, schooling, and future he will put forth the same effort into his relationship. His efforts will be remarkably unmatchable. He will do things for you that you could have never imagined a man would do and he will never let you down and will always be there for you through anything. He will have all the attributes of what a good man is supposed to be. He will be as honorable, noble, and as loyal as any man can get. Without any distractions he will have the majority of his time to devote to you and if you can appreciate what he has become, a queen is what you will become in his eyes and being his queen comes with a vast number of rewards and benefits. There will be the occasional everyday distractions like work, friends, and family but that will not take away the joy and the love he has in his heart for you.

THE STAND-UP GUY

This is one of the guys everybody enjoys and loves to have around. He is well-rounded, has a good structured upbringing, and is as dependable as they come. He is this way, not because he tries to, it's just the way he is and it shows with everything he does. This is the guy that is a favorite at all the parties and is calm, cool, and collected enough to take to your job's yearly picnic or your family reunion and no one will have anything bad to say about him. This is the respectable one, no matter what is going on he can find something good out of any unstable situation. He can learn to smile despite the horrible things life can bring his way. The hardships of every day living doesn't tarnish the shimmer of the shine he possesses. This guy can be sometimes called "the good guy" of any relationship and is as compromising as they get. He holds something in his heart a lot of men don't have and that is honor. He "honors thy mother and thy father" but more important he has learned to honor his woman and his family and in his life.

The stand-up guy has morals about himself and, regardless of what he is faced with, he thinks things through just to make sure it is done in a manner that reflects who he is. Within this thinking process, it allows him to take the proper actions necessary to tackle all of the issues of the day. He is the one that makes the least amount of mistakes because of this thinking and his ability to process each situation. This guy is the one you can leave your kids around and know they will be well taken care of in your absence. He is the one your mom will like because he doesn't try too hard to be something he isn't. You see the impression he leaves with everyone stands out and sticks to their memory. He is just this good of a guy, he doesn't do much out of character. He is who he is every time you see him. No matter the mood, the time of day, or what he is going through every time he sees you, he treats you the same way.

This is the guy that brings life to whatever he touches. He has a nurturing hand that causes everything around him to grow. He has a gleam about himself that lights up a room when he walks in. Ladies, you know this guy when you see him its like he is walking with his own spotlight that follows him wherever he goes. You know the one where this is so often said, "There is just something about him." He just passes the test of being who he is and only who he is. He doesn't try to be anything but the guy you met the first day you saw him and stays in character from that day on without distraction or disruption. But the main reason why I call him the stand-up guy is because of the morals he lives by. He will never cross you in any way. He will be there for you if you really need him and if you ever make it to the point to where he sees you as a good friend, he will always be by your side no matter what turns your relationship may take. Even if you break up, he will still be one of the best friends you will ever come across and you can call and count on him to do the right thing by you, sometimes without question. He is just a good, genuine guy.

LIAR, LIAR

Oh my, you know this one. He is the guy no matter the subject he has a really good lie to make his story sound just that much better than yours and will over-exaggerate every story he tells. This guy is known for going over the top with no matter how thick the story has been laid on before him. This is the price for laying it on thick or the king of misrepresentation. No matter how good your trip, your story, your party, or just your life is, his is always going to be the one to exceed all others. I think we all know a guy of this type because he has this annoying habit of getting on everyone's nerves with all the lies.

Normally, this may not be the worst of men to get involved with but if you want reliability and honesty out of your man, stay clear of the liar. He makes his life and everything about him seem so much more glamorous than what it really is and may degrade others in the process. Don't forget you still have the good potential to lead your relationship and if you can get him out of this childish phase he is in, he can be bred into a different and sometimes better person. But if that is not what he is looking for, stay as far away from this little liar bug before he gets you trapped in his web of deceit. And you have to realize you will almost never be able to trust a word that comes out of his mouth.

Sometimes the problem with this guy is he doesn't realize he is the problem of his own life. I am not saying he doesn't know he is lying because he spends too much time imagining some of the things he comes up with. It's just seems as though he doesn't realize the lying is why people have a habit of avoiding him at times. For him, friends are so hard to come by especially when no one can tell when they are being told the truth. Most people can't stand being lied to by anyone but by people they hold close to them really hurts. This is why this guy is normally a loner, not by choice of course, but it's truly by force he loves his own company more than others do. But when dealing with him, the worse case scenario is that this guy can be one of those compulsive liars. One of those people that gets so rapped up in those lies he believes them. If honesty is a priority of yours this will not ever be the man for you.

THE PLAYBOY

This is the one that all the girls love but he is the one that will hurt their hearts the most. He is the smooth, clean-cut, and good-looking guy that ladies will find themselves falling for. This guy has all the attributes to be the best man a woman would want to have in her life. With this guy there is only one problem, he willingly makes himself available to other women. He doesn't want to settle down with anyone. He is here for his own personal pleasures and that is it. It hurts the women he comes into contact with because they want so much from him but he just can't be what they want him to be because he doesn't have it in him. He can't seem to let go of his own selfishness and the lifestyle he has built. He would probably be one of the best men any woman can come across but he is not here for her but for his own enjoyment and pleasures.

For the life of me, I can't figure out why women want so much from him. It seems as though even when women know they can not have him and he shows them he doesn't want them, ladies still try and force him to be with them but it never works. If he shows you in any way he is not the one you want him to be it may be time to start looking for someone else to invest your time in. There are certain characteristics you have to look for and certain signs you have to watch for. With this one you have to be very careful simply because he will fool you into thinking you are so special and if it seems too good to be true, the majority of the time it is. Watch for the unanswered calls, the unadulterated lies why he couldn't make it, all the girls who are just friends, and if you are a little too curious, you will find a lot more than you bargain for so be careful in your investigation.

There are things about this guy that go overlooked for a number of years for a number of reasons. Whether it is love which is blinding your judgment or it is something else, it still gets looked over. When your emotions get in the way when you're going through the relationship phase you sometimes miss some of the key signs that will help prevent hurt when you come to that fork in the road that leads to a lot of heartache and pain because he will give it to you if you set yourself up for failure. The failure comes in to play when you actually know better but don't do better. You know when he is not for you and has done things time after time to hurt your heart and you look these situations over and make up an excuse for why it is happening. Even though you want to confront him about the problems at hand but that feeling of loneliness is what keeps you from getting the answers you desire. In your times of hurt the same question gets asked, "Why do the cute guys always come with the most problems?"

MR. OHH WEE

This guy is the one every lady loves but sometimes don't know how to treat him and maybe its because of some of the hang-ups he has. This is the one, no matter how you are feeling and no matter the time of the day or night, he comes through and puts it down just the way you like it. His name will vary, no matter how long you go in life or how far you move away, you will never forget how he treated your body. He holds you like no other, he squeezes you like you have never been touched before, and he kisses you in a way no one has ever thought to and he does this with the utmost regard to you and that's what turns you on. Can you imagine a thought that seems so familiar and so different at the same time? Has someone had a hold on you that you don't know how to control? He will work your body like a full time job.

This is the guy that gives you the feeling that helps you to overlook most of the flaws he has because he is spectacular in bed. This guy is better than the best you have ever had. He is the one the bar was broken on. He does the heavy lifting. He takes control of the situation and has his way with your body but he does so with the simple task of just listening to your every wish. This is what he is good at and he does it without hesitation. There is nothing he doesn't know about you because you didn't have to tell him but once and he made mental notes. With the other things he has learned during the time he has spent with you, only compliment the way he has learned to treat your body.

This is not a tough task but when your man doesn't pay the proper attention he needs to, he misses out on some of the most important qualities you have to offer. These qualities I speak of are some of the most beautiful parts of a woman. Something as simple as putting a smile on your loved ones faces is a remarkable thing to see. The hard part about having a real relationship with this guy is he has all the qualities you desire out of your man in the bedroom, it is just he lacks some of the other important qualities of a man you are looking for. The responsibilities, the quality working man, family values, or whatever it is he is lacking in important areas. He is what he is and that is a bedroom toy and nothing more. And no matter how much you want for him to be the man you want him to be, he continues to let you down simply because you continue to let him in.

MR. UNAVAILABLE

This is the guy you talk to on an occasional basis and it seems he is a nice or good enough guy to date or get to know but it seems impossible to get him in any one place alone at any time. He may just have a lot going on in his life which doesn't include you. He may not be trying to be difficult with you he has too much to deal with and having you wouldn't seem like a bad idea but there aren't enough hours in the day to have you the way you want him. No matter how many missed phone calls, all the shortened conversations, or even the promises that keep getting broken which lead to misguided thoughts. The type of thoughts that lead you to believe there is something wrong with you and those thoughts may or may not affect your thinking of what it is you are doing wrong, when you are not the defining issue but he is.

Don't take him the wrong way. He is just the type of guy that has issues that direct his attention into a different direction. He may not want to hurt you or set you up for another bad relationship. He just cannot be there for you like you want him to be and depending on the issues he has he may not ever find the time for you. The buttons he push sets you off in an interesting way to the point to where you are made to be overwhelmed with who he is. The unknown is the thing that may set you off about this mysterious man. Sometimes the unknown is a good thing and for others it can be some of the most heartbreaking times you have ever seen in your life. Simply because no matter how much you reach out to him he doesn't reach back.

You sometimes have to use your better judgment to figure out it may just be something simple that is keeping him from giving you the attention you desire. He just may be hiding something and what he is hiding is something you may not want to know. There are a number of reasons that will keep a man out of your reach. One of them is he has a working relationship or is married and doesn't have the time for another active relationship. The reasons why men lie is to keep you at bay when things get a little rough at home and he will use you to satisfy his desires when his other half will not. In a man's eyes, he likes it when women like him. He uses that to his advantage and drags on a relationship with them knowing there will never be a future for one.

For whatever the reason, this guy is not the relationship guy you are looking for. If you think about it, he may already be in a relationship and that's why he cannot make himself available for you and what you want him for. Whether he is married, already has a girlfriend, or just a family situation that doesn't give him the time to deal with you. Maybe his job keeps him busy working long hours and his personal life takes the back seat. Then there is his wife and his two kids that are so time consuming he doesn't seem to want to engage in another relationship that may cause problems along the line with the family he has groomed to be his own.

Then again it may be something as simple as you not being the type of woman he desires to have in his life. No matter the reason you come up with, just remember that when you and him don't hit it off like you would like to, be happy because he could have strung you along and led you to believe you could have been the one and really hurt your feelings. Just be happy and look at it like this, you can never miss what you never had but we can always wonder.

THE LEACH

Last but not least I would like to introduce you to the slimy, little leach. This is the man who I like to call, worthless. It's not that he is not a good man but he has a very long history of not doing a damn thing with his time. This is the guy that no matter what is going on he will find a reason not to make it happen. No matter the adjective you use to describe him, he is the man that doesn't seem to be worthy of being called a man. Whether you think he is lazy, no good, or just down right trifling he does fit the bill. This is one of the guys you wish you never met.

With the thought of a few "get rich" scheme that never seem to end well. A bundle of jobs which don't ever seem to last as long as they should. This is the man that will sit around and watch his woman go to work and will bring her lunch to your job but won't take the time to come in and fill out an application. But he will sit at home playing the video game, at your house with his friends drinking, or just sitting around shooting the breeze all day while you are hard at work. This is the man that will have his woman snatching patches of hair out of your head because he has good intentions, but does nothing with them. He frustrates you so much because he has all of the physical and mental capabilities to be one of the most productive men you have met but it seems as though he is somewhat happy with the situation he is in. He is happy with you taking care of him, he is content with not being able to do for himself or the family he has.

The strange part of this is he may have a skill that can keep him with work but for some reason or another he can't hold down a job. This is where the frustration comes from when you know he can do better but he doesn't. He seems to be content with everyone around him having nice things and growing into successful people. You know the guy that I am speaking of, the one that will stand around doing nothing but waiting on the opportunity for someone to do something for him. This is one of the worst kinds of men that walk this planet. He is unlike any self-respecting man I have ever run across. Most real men won't take handouts. This man will and he will take it a level further, he has fixed his mouth to ask for handouts from everyone he feels would say yes. I feel that any service that is provided by a man is to be compensated financially to that man if that is what is agreed on before that service is rendered. The problem with this type of man is that no matter how he conducts himself or the favors he asks he will never be able to do the same in return because how can you pay back anything when you have nothing and how will you repay a favor when you are too lazy to do so. It just doesn't make any sense. There are times when we all fall into a rut and it seems we can't get out of but this man learns to live there and live there comfortably.

TRUST

In the animal kingdom trust has to be earned and the trust of the most dominant has to be taken by a show of mostly brute force in order to set dominance. Animals live like this because they are in the wild and they have to be able to set the rules of the kingdom seemingly through force only. We as people don't have to live like that because we are supposed to be able to communicate and work our way through our problems without resorting to violence. Although we as human beings are supposed to be the smartest of the animals in this kingdom, there is a lot that can be learned about ourselves with watching other animals. Even though most of us don't look at ourselves as animals, we are and we still have the instincts of one. When something doesn't feel right we react according to the situation. The animal in us is what helps us to make certain changes, decisions, or even helps us to choose our mates. Because the strength of a person will determine if they will be in our life and how long they will be there. We all have to make sure the person we are with is there for us.

The same instinct that drives the lion to attack its prey or the instinct of a mother bird to push her young out of the nest for the first time is similar to the type of instinct that drives us as humans. A man instinctively finds a way to woo a woman with no idea of what attracts him to her. This drive allows us to make decisions in our lives to stop doing things that don't help a relationship prosper is the driving force of our beings. Before the lion can lead his pack, he has to build a pack. He has to know without a shadow of a doubt he can trust the pack to hunt, feed the young, and breed with. The same trust that puts him at the head of his pack, knowing there are so many dangers out there. Even though the dangers of a relationship are not as detrimental to our survival but the pain which comes with some of the heartaches can be just as dangerous.

For most of us, male and female alike, trust is a real touchy topic. We all have trust issues that only time has a factor in changing. We all have been through our share of ups and downs that helped or hurt our perception of what a real trustworthy person is. Our different views are what makes this such a controversial subject. This is what causes us to react to the different trials and tribulations of our everyday lives. As hard as this subject is to discuss I am going to tackle it as hard as I can because we all need to hear about it to help us understand it a little more so we can grow together and not just individually. Because the actions of men are so misunderstood we sometimes need a little help with the frequently asked question of "Why?"

The *why* may turn out to be the unseen variable that doesn't rear its head up until after the act is committed without understanding. Most people don't take out the time to evaluate themselves and why different situations keep happening to them. If we all get to the point where we learn what it takes to satisfy our own desires first, we will have a happier, healthier and less stressful life. Majority of the time it is not a why that we need to be asking. We need to go a little deeper instead of just scratching the surface of the problem. The surfaces is the why but the real question needs to be, why was this person so comfortable with doing what they did?

In reading this, I would like for you to take the time and make a list of the things in your life that truly make you happy and it doesn't make a difference how small it may seem to you put it on the list. After you have made your list, be sure to put it up in a place you can get to it at a later date. Give yourself about two months or maybe longer and go back to the list just so I can help you do a little experiment. When you decide to go back to it ask yourself. "Has anything changed?"

That's the thing that most people don't take out the time to pay attention to. All things change in time including our wants, needs and desires. So the same thing you enjoyed yesterday may not bring you the same pleasures tomorrow and this is what the experiment is for. And the subject of trust for men works out the same way and as the time passes and we evolve over that time. The things we trust in will eventually change, just like the way the time changes so does everything else.

The issue of trust has been very argumentative and a lot of relationships have suffered from this because it is hard for most people to understand the meaning of this word varies from individual to individual. It has been said there is nothing worse than a woman scorned. They may be right. On the other hand, there is nothing harsher than a man with a broken heart. After this man is hurt, it is difficult for him to learn to trust again and he can grow to be so cold to the women in his life. Can you imagine living your life with someone who is just going through the motions of living and not wanting to change or enjoy their life? His heart can grow to be as cold as a polar bear's toe nail in an Antarctic winter. When he is hurt it is too hard for him to bounce back. When coming back after a heartbreak a man will never be the same and his views of life are different. This can be the making of a monster of the worst kind simply because he will grow to be the bitterest old man ever seen. Bouncing from one angry moment to the next. When it comes to dealing with the ladies of his life it will lead to a long line of misunderstandings that end with unanswered questions. Some situations that could have been avoided but the bitterness in this man's heart will not let him be as understanding about small issues in his life. This is why those small issues grow into big problems that ultimately end up in a heated breakup. This happens time and time again and without the proper help, this guy will hurt plenty women. Those of which are just looking for someone to love and someone to love them with the same love they put out.

For the unsettled mind this will help you grasp the concept of what it is to be trusted by men of all types. A man can love you and not trust you but it is impossible for a man to trust you and not love you. This may seem to be disturbing but the statement is true. It happens every day and it is hard to picture being with someone who thinks this way and you may be laying with this man right now. This is not going to change no matter how hard you try and the harder you try, the more you fail.

It's not your fault but it will seem that way because you will continue to attempt to reach him and all of your efforts will not be enough. This person you are dealing with is so caught up within himself your feelings and your desires take the back seat to whatever it is he's dealing with. The more you try the more it seems you push him away. You may try and rationalize what is going wrong and the frustrations of trying to do so only end up in another breakup. Sometimes you have to remember there are some men out there you will never reach and you have to stop trying so hard. If you are something he desires to have he will come to you and meet you on an even playing field with a open line of communication to solve any problems.

This is mainly because most women try to do the one thing that will push most men away. Women try to change their man. Some women do this without regard to the man and how he feels and some do this unconsciously. Sometimes you push and don't know that you're pushing but this open the door for issues. This excessive pushing gets to be nerve-wrecking the harder the pushing gets. (Remember this push because it will come up again.) Most men don't take kindly to being pushed and rushed into situations that may bring negative changes into their lives. The last thing any man needs or desires is someone trying to think for him or intervene on the issues of his life. He knows right from wrong, or so he thinks. Most men left their mothers at her house and came out into this world trying to build a future of their own. All the trials and tribulations he goes through are the reasons why he treats people the way he does and how he trusts the people in his life. When you know who you are dealing with it is a little less complicated to deal with the person who you are trying to give your heart to.

One of the issues of trust men have with women is most women don't realize trust has to be earned through trials which have their time periods. It doesn't have a designated hour, month or year where he can say, "In a week or so he will let down his guards and we will be able to move to the next stage of our relationship." No, it's not like that at all. This period varies from person to person because it depends on the hardships this man has been through in his life from the loss of his first love up to now.

There are a few different variables that affect a man and how he deals with the trials of his life. Most men have been hurt at least once in his lifetime and with this hurt comes a time of grieving to get over whatever the situation was. Just like any other person we all need time to figure out what the next step of your life will be. Not just the next step of our lives but the next step for our hearts. During this transition is the time a man close himself off from the world, while trying to protect his heart.

No matter how tough or strong a man seems to be on the outer appearance, he is motivated completely by the strength of his heart. When his heart gets cold he may become difficult to deal with. The longer his heart has been cold, the further away from love this man is and the harder it is going to be to reach him on a level of love. You may think it is impossible to reach him but it isn't. Trying to pull him back into love will be a long, hard journey which many women are not willing to travel. Simply because the journey gets to be tiresome and can be too stressful for most.

One of the tricky things about trust comes along with love and its belief. The belief that someone can learn to love you as much as you can learn to love yourself. A person who will treat you better than you will treat your own body and heart. This is where the problem comes in, we have a hard time finding something or someone we can believe in. Our faith in the unknown gets really hard to explain because we put so much into what it is we see and not enough into what we feel. Can you believe there is someone out there who will put as much time into you as you do? Is there a person who will invest the time and energy into your relationship you will? Can someone care as much as you do about the issues of your life and help keep you moving on with your day to day living? Do you think there is someone out there like that? There are people out there but the hard part about it all is learning not to settle for less than you know you're worth.

Sometimes it is difficult for us to believe in something or someone other than ourselves and this is why our hearts are so troubled at times. We take the little this world gives us and we adjust our minds into thinking this is somehow the best we can get. This compulsiveness is what gets us stuck because as we get adjusted to not having what we mostly desire, we spend more time missing out on some of the greater pleasures of life. The happiness and the joys of finding many different reasons for smiling that come along with living a happy and healthy life with someone we love and loves us completely. This comes along with not catching the right fish or not using the right bait for the right catch. Sometimes when life gets a tad bit hard and you go through a few difficult phases in your life, you have a tendency to take in strays cats and dogs who are not up to the standard you set. At this particular time, this turns out to be the right person for the job of being the comforter. You may not have thought this situation would work but it was just something about them that stood out and grabbed your attention at that particular time.

It may not have been anything spectacular like the quality of their conversation. They saw your defenses were down and decided to go for it because the time seemed right. But blindly going through the motions sets us up for failure and we don't realize our mistakes until it is too late. Let's say you have moved in together, have built a life together, or have gotten married and have a child or two. It's at this point you realize you have out-grown this person you are with and now you want out and you don't understand how that worked out to be so.

That goes back to the list and evolving because you're ready for the next chapter in the book of your life and they are content with the way things are. But you have to do what you can to get your significant other to get on the same page you are on. If not, just get him to read the same book. That goes back to the person you were and the person you desire to become. The more you mature into the being you are growing in to the more you want out of life and if the person you are with isn't cutting it there will be a separation notice coming in the mail really soon.

During our evolving stages there comes times when we question our trust and how we handle each situation we come in contact with. If everyone thought the same way the world would be a much more enjoyable place to live. Since everyone has the right to agree to disagree, we are left in a world where everyone has their own opinion and thinks their way is the right way. This difference in opinion is what causes the arguments. When the arguments get started there is a separation of power because the people involved stand behind what they believe is true. Now they are at odds with each other and no one wants to admit they were wrong or maybe they weren't looking at it from the other person's perspective. You know if you wrote the number 6 down on a piece of paper and sat it in the middle of a table and your partner sat across from you, they would see something different. It is the same thing but depending on your outlook at that moment it is different.

The hardest part about trust for any man is opening up and entrusting his heart to someone who could eventually break it again. For the ladies who read this, you have to understand giving up his heart to you is the one most difficult tasks he will ever do to show you he loves you. If he has been hurt in his past this makes it just that much more difficult for him to do. For any man to tell you he loves you and does everything he can to prove it this should not be taken likely. To abuse the kindness of this man's heart this may drive him crazy and hurt him in a way it makes it difficult for him to heal. This is where the crazy guy sometimes comes from.

Some people are just naturally unstable and have had problems all their lives but this crazy guy I speak of is made to be this way by the women in his life who have hurt him. Some woman in his past, whether it was his mother or the love of his life who took his heart and squeezed it until there wasn't an ounce of love left. Women have a tendency of opening up quicker to other relationships and forgiving so they can move on but its not like that with guys. That's why most men keep their hearts locked away and rarely pulls it out again. This is where the "dog" comes into play.

This dog is what most women try their best to avoid. He is cunning and he doesn't care about who he hurts while he is on his tantrum. That ice cold heart shows up and continues to show as he bounces from person to person. At this point this dog can't be tamed. He goes through the motions giving women the impression he cares when it is the total opposite. During this time he is more trouble than he is worth. But there is a flip side to this process. He's a dog yes but he still desires to have someone he can call his own. He has a desire to change but he has to want to change and this change is sparked by a woman who has attributes that he likes and she sparks an interest in him that opens him up. You don't have to go out of your way to show him you are not like the ladies of his past. You just have to continue to be yourself because establishing your own identity is a priceless quality in any man's eyes. This allows for him to open up and trust you the way you want him to. You have to comprehend no matter how your relationship is going, being honest and genuine to yourself first and then to him helps those defensive walls fall one at a time.

When those walls come down and you start to really enjoy each other for all you are worth and life seems much more pleasant. So when you enjoy the man he enjoys the woman and when a man enjoys his woman he is in his royalty stage where you go from being the lady friend in his life to his queen. Regardless of what your flaws are, he sees right passed them and only sees you, someone who can become the love of his life.

Just do yourself a favor and don't rush it because if you haven't made it to this point the only thing you can do to create a problem with this process is try and press the issue. No man likes to be forced into anything, especially a relationship of any kind. The level of commitment it takes to make a relationship work comes in time. That level of commitment and trust has to come from his heart and he has to be ready for it, if not there is nothing you can do to change his mind.

When you try to force a man into something he isn't ready for he has a tendency to get defensive or he has a tendency to run. When he feels he isn't ready for the responsibilities he will cower out of the relationship. Since he is not man enough to take on the issues presented before him he will use this as an excuse to wonder into the arms of another woman. With this compulsive attitude he will do everything to flip the situation and try make it seem as though the it is you. Some men will outgrow this juvenile mentality. But for some this will be a repeating theme in their lives because when situations of this caliber arise they will revert back to the only thing they know.

There is no real schedule that men go by. He doesn't look at the calendar and say on the twenty-third of May I will tell her I love her and on the thirtieth of November I may ask her to marry me. It is not like that, not like that at all. No man likes to be pressured into anything especially when it has to deal with his heart and if there is any chance of him getting his heart hurt, he will pull a cowardly lion and tuck tail and run. So when you push he pushes back now you have a full-fledged game of tug-of-war because every time you pull, he pulls and no one actually wins because no one is truly happy with the outcome of the situation. The beautiful part of it all, when he finally stops running and he is open to allow himself into his life and heart you no longer have to try to force anything because it will come to you.

You have to look outside the box sometimes to understand the reason why men do things the way they do them. If you are pushing him to do something you have to understand that men are creatures of reasoning. In the back of his mind he is asking himself, "What exactly are her motives for doing what she is doing?" He may not ask in that form but he does ask. So he starts to watch you to see what your motives are to ease his mind if not only for a little self-gratification. And this is a testimony of the trust that you have built with him and at this point he knows he is being tested, but the reason why is hard for him to figure out. Sometime the pressure of trying to satisfy a woman can get to be a little more than most men can bear. The responsibility of the job at hand is more than he expected or he may not feel he is qualified for that position. When he feels it is too much for him to handle he will start to shy away from you and he will not answer all of your calls or he may come up with different reasons why he can't come to see you and the distance he is putting between you is sometimes permanent because of the type of person he is.

Even though the privacy act doesn't include your relationship and it should. His e-mails and cell phone may be the best way to find out if he is doing something outside of the relationship but this violates the trust in the relationship. You have to be careful and you have to be aware what you find may crush you and change your opinion of him. The problem with this type situation is that it causes tension in the relationship. If he was doing what he was supposed to be doing you wouldn't have to worry about this being an issue. The only thing that I can say is for you to be careful the next time you want to do some investigating. Also make sure that you are strong enough to handle what you find because it may hurt you more than you know. Not just hurt you it is going to hurt the stability of your relationship. Let's just say you don't find anything. How do you bounce back as a couple after you have shown signs of there being trust issues on your end?

In life, there are some things you have to understand about men and one of them is that most men are creatures of habit. They follow a daily routine they learn to follow. Anything done outside of the box is unexpected and is sometimes unwanted because it is uncomfortable for most. Sometimes when you feel like bringing up a subject that may cause an argument, it would be a good idea to pick your fights as they come. What I mean by this is occasionally when you want to pick a fight or take up matters about an issue it is a good idea to get a feel for how he is feeling. When it comes to matters of the heart some issues can't wait, because if you have a no-good, cheating man and you just found out about his affairs, it is a good idea to go ahead and take care of that because that can easily turn ugly for the both of you.

On the other hand, if he is a good guy and came in a little late I say get a good feel for how he comes in because anything could have happened between the time he left from where he was and to the time when he finally made it home. A series of unfortunate circumstances could have changed his whole world on his way home. Like I say, sometimes the full court pressure is necessary but you have to be able to determine when it is time to put it into action.

This is a part of compromising we have to go through to make sure our relationship works out for the better. This way you will have less stress-filled days. Most arguments always travel the path as if it were a comet. It flies on and on until it finally comes in contact with something in its path to crash into. When that comet of anger finally crashes it will burn as long as you allow it and the longer you let the fire from the crash fester the worse things will get so dash a little conversation on it to calm the flame.

Remember: The first thing about trust is it has to be earned and we all know this. After the man in your life can show you that you can trust in him, that's when things will work out for the best. You have to stay away from the things men say and look more into the things they do because a man's actions are always genuine. He will do everything he can do to show you he is there for you and will not hesitate to do so. You have to understand he is looking for a few characteristics in you for this to work. He is looking for his better half to complement him. Someone he can find peace in, someone who he can share his dreams with and build them with; and more importantly, someone he can trust to love him unconditionally through all of the ups and downs. No man wants to leave home with his cape on to take on the world on a daily basis and return home to have to continue to fight.

CHEATING

This is the chapter most women want to hear about because it happens so often. With everything that is going on in your life, between work, school, and your social life this situation in your relationship will have you pulling your hair out. So before you have to set an appointment with your local psychiatrist allow me to enlighten you on some of the things you will go through because of us men. I know you have to deal with a lot already and dealing with men adds on to the stressful life you already live. The trouble with understanding us when we do certain things is we don't understand ourselves. Depending on the circumstances that present themselves we don't have a clue until we sit down and think about it and this is the problem with most men, they don't think first. No one deserves to have their heart hurt in this way and even though it happens it is still wrong on his part and wrong to you.

There are a number of different speculations out there that have been said about the reasons why men cheat, and some of them make a lot of sense if you took the time to look deeper into what really goes on. There are a number of different factors that determine the outcome of a man cheating. Some of the issues will come about simply because men have a tendency to act off of impulse without thinking. Some say men have a cheater gland in their body which causes them to cheat. It is not the gland that pushes men to cheat it is a number of other variables which lead up to it.

It's kind of difficult for most to understand that sometimes it is not the man's fault he is the cheater he is. I am not trying to take up for some of the mishaps men go though or some of the weaknesses men have but there are some weak men who fall for whatever comes their way. Sometimes you have to look somewhere outside of the proverbial box to really get a good picture of how and why things periodically turn out the way that they do.

The Dog, as men are called majority of the time, is really a dog and there is no changing him. He lives by the standard of what society has taught him. This double standard which figuratively says it is a part of a man's nature to cheat. Family and society tells us it is good for a man to sow his oats. So when asked about their sexual exploits most men can't even explain why they went through with the act. You have to acknowledge most men don't have the capability to properly express themselves in a manner that is satisfactory for you. Even when simple situations are presented men seem to have the toughest time communicating these issues.

There are a few factors that lead up to a man cheating and the most important factor is the strength of that man. This factor really depends on the man simply because if he isn't strong enough to fight off the demons he likes, he will fall for them every single time. Even though he wants to do well and wants everything to work out for the best in your relationship if he can't fight off the things that turn him on, he will stray and he won't be able to stop himself from making some of the biggest mistakes of his life.

This is the fact every man can attest to. The fact that when he is trying to do better by the relationship he is in that's when all his old mistresses come out of the woodwork and when it seems like every woman he meets wants a piece of him. Like the scenario after a man gets married. It seems as though the wedding ring attracts women to him. Truth of the matter is, women sometimes prey on men who are married because they don't plan to build an attachment to this man. It may be for the challenge to see if she can get him to cheat or just the idea of being able to take the happiness he has and destroying it.

In this day and time women are a lot more aggressive than they used to be so it may be the fact he has someone at this time, it may be the thrill of the chase for women or for whatever the reason, it comes to him from all directions. Most people can't stand it when you are happy and like that old saying goes, "Misery loves company." This is when the strength of your man is tested to the fullest. Have you ever thought about different situations your man has to face on a daily basis? They are much like what you go through but on a different level and on a different playing field. In your game, when you meet a man and he is the aggressor you have the upper hand, but when a man is being pursued by a woman his options are limited and will be looked at differently by his peers. If he says no this act can be frowned upon by those of weaker minds.

If he is as strong as he should be he will sit back and evaluate the situation so he can make sure he keeps all of his ducks in a row and say no to the proposals presented before him. If he is of any weak standards he will give in. Even though he will have his doubts and his regrets about what he has done, in the end he has still cheated.

This is the perfect time to bring a few things to your attention you may not know or may not care to pay attention to. Let's just say it is his ex-girlfriend and she has started making different advances at him again and some of them are sexual. You don't understand the type of pressure this puts a man under. It is easy to suggest he should say no but until you have seen some of the things women do to get a man's attention, then you'll understand. You as a woman should already understand this because when you have your eyes set on someone there is no limit to the things you will do to get him and make him yours. Some will fight tooth and nail to get what they want and some will even tell some of the most convening lies they can think of.

If she is an ex she already knows what it is he likes, more importantly what he dislikes or what his personal preferences are. Can you imagine trying to fight off someone who may know you better than you know yourself sometimes? I ask this simply because women are so observant on all levels. From the clothes he likes, to the way he likes his dinner cooked, to the warmth of his bath water. You will learn all these things when you are with a man. Cheating will always be a problem for most relationships because of the different variables that can present themselves. The biggest problem comes when men can't learn to think more with the head that's on their shoulders.

There is a real level of difficulty that comes with a man being able to just say no. Believe it or not his reason for saying no is set in his heart more so than his mind. If he can sit back and contemplate on how much him saying no will help him more so than it would hurt you this will take him a long way. This sense of clarity comes with experience and an inexperienced man will foul this up every time. Most people have yet to understand the concept this I speak of. It is not only you that helps him to determine if he is going to go outside of the relationship and deal with someone else. There are a few important questions he asks himself and sometimes he answers himself to help him to decide if he is willing to stray. The questions don't necessarily have an order but they are asked. Is she really worth the headache? Can I keep this a secret? Is she worth me loosing everything that I already have? There are a few more questions that may come to mind but there should be one question of concern. What are the motives of this person?

The act of cheating isn't evaluated by men before they do it, they don't prepare themselves for the issues to come. The headaches that may come in with dealing with her on a regular basis. No matter the relationship men have with women, when it turns sexual, women have a tendency to demand more time because their feelings will eventually get deeply involved. When a woman has put her heart into a situation with a man, it is hard to let go. This is when the discrepancies of a man's scheduling and habits change. He has to find ways to compensate for the time needed to keep and ongoing relationship with this other woman. At this point the frequent phone calls begin to occur. Never ending text messages that may cause for him to silence his phone.

Now while she is trying to get your man's attention, there has to be a reason for that. In the beginning, her motives may not come out but before everything is said and done her motives will come out. She may be pushing at him simply because she doesn't like you and she wants to be able to say she has had your man. She may see the potential in him that you have looked over. She might just be attracted to him and its strictly about sex. The questions about a woman's motives can go on and on but let me get back to this writing.

Men find it hard to tell women no for some reason or another. Even though he may know dealing with this woman or this type of woman is not a good feel for him he can't for the life of him fight the temptation. The temptation is not just from him. It's the way society is set up the more women a man sleeps with he is considered a stud but if a woman does the same thing she is thought of in another manner. It is more so an ego boost for him to do so. The boost comes in when he discusses the different scenarios with his friends and he listens to them and their silly opinions of the situations of his life.

82 | JAWORSKI D. COFFEY

In every man's mind he wants to be the playboy type at least once in his life. What man wouldn't want to be the 2022version of the Hugh Hefner? Who wouldn't want to be that guy? If you listened to the ways of today's society it is good to be that guy and a lot of guys I know would love to be that guy. Most men wouldn't kill to walk in the footsteps of Mr. H. Hefner. Most of these guys are nothing like they lead you to believe. Even though most men want to be Hef they don't understand this is his lifestyle. This is his means of income and this is why he lives like this. Most men will never get the chance to reach this level. Only a selected few will get a chance to see this lifestyle in person. Hef is a businessman first. But the idea of being something you're not makes it hard for guys to be themselves because if you looked at it from the outside looking in this type of guy always gets the girl.

Even though he may have the strength to say no he may be somewhat reluctant of doing the right thing. There are a few factors that add to the hindering or the helping of this action. His reluctance is mostly determined by what you actually mean to him. If you have not had the best of relationships and have been on the rocks, you can almost make a guarantee he will go astray as soon as the opportunity presents itself. Not trying to shift the blame but some men are just looking for a way out. Too cowardly to stand up and be a man and tell you how he truly feels.

At this point he is surely tired of what you have been through and even though leaving would be his best option but in his mind, unconsciously, he is afraid. Either afraid to step up or afraid of the idea of having to let go of the situation he has gotten so acquainted with. Now he is so delusional where he doesn't take responsibility for what he has done, so he shifts the blame on his woman. Not because he has cheated but because you haven't been doing what he feels you should have. If you are lacking in any area of your relationship to him this is the best reason to cheat and ladies you have to remember no matter what you will or will not do there is a woman out there that will. Even though he doesn't know what he wants you suffer behind his action. When things have gotten to this point, he has lost all respect for you, your relationship, and everything you have worked so hard to build. Your relationship will eventually shatter like a brick smashing a threw windshield.

A man's reluctance depends strictly on how happy they are with the situation they are in. People have their own interpretation of what happiness is. To go deeper into this, most don't have a clue of what it takes to stay happy. Some will try to force happiness but forcing it will never work.

Sometimes the problem with this is most women don't know when to let up and this can drive a man somewhere near crazy. Most men know women have to have the last word on everything but with a combination of life, love, finance, and friendship can weigh in heavy on a man as time goes on. The wear and tear of dealing with relationship problems have a way of driving people away and I don't mean just your man. After a while the people who you hold near and dear to you will start to shy away from you when you become the damper of the party. Sometimes just knowing when to be quiet can save your relationship.

Everything doesn't have to be an argument and everything you hear doesn't have to be discussed either. After information has been passed on to you, it should be evaluated first. If it holds any weight on your life share it and if not keep it to yourself. Sometimes information given to you is used to upset you and try to come into play inside of your relationship. Occasionally people tell you things to try and wedge their way into your personal life and disrupt your life. If your relationship is good, is going in the right direction, built on common ground, and you are happy with what you have, be sure you don't allow your friends or your family to dictate the direction of your relationship. The majority of the time, your friends can be the best things in the world to have but sometimes they can bring you the worst pain when the only thing they think they are doing is helping but attempting to help can present problems in your relationship.

The biggest misunderstandings you may have with your mate is when you put the words of others before you put the trust of theirs. Your true friends will be there for you through thick and thin. The one other thing friends will do no matter what is do their best to protect you. In the process of protecting you they sometimes put themselves in bad positions. One of those positions is when they feel they are doing you a favor by coming to you and relaying information they have heard or seen about your mate. Some married couples who have been together for a long period of time say you have to be able to try to keep the relationship between husband and friends somewhat separate. I know its easier said than done but it is possible. Because combining the two can bring unwanted stress on both. In most healthy relationships there is a level of privacy that keeps things running well.

Do you know what's worse than lying, deceiving or cheating? Nothing, they are all intertwined with one and other in the same web. The one thing a person can do to end any friendship of any kind, is show distrust or betrayal. Almost anything else can be forgiven. However when the trust of a relationship has been broken there is almost no turning back. Even though all things can be forgiven, this is the hardest to forget. Just he idea of betrayal can cause a relationship to fall apart. This is a feeling that burns so deep it burns all the way to the core. To go against the grain hurts the moral fiber that relationships of all kind are built. It doesn't have to be a relationship between a man and a woman but it can be a relationship between brothers which can be broken by one person's action of unfaithfulness. The act of this magnitude can and will destroy anything you have built in the relationship. It hurts so much because it comes from one of the people you have committed all of your trust into. One of the closest people you thought would never do that to you. And when it does happen it feels like a flaming dagger cutting through your heart through your back and it only gets hotter the longer it stays in.

The ability to keep people out of your business is one of the hardest things to do. Simply because you want to believe in them and you trust their judgment on the matters of your life. But like any responsible adult should do is to let the inquiries of others stay where they are and that is outside the walls of your home. Once the issues and the opinion of others are brought into your home, this disrupts the flow of your relationship.

It is good to take the information in but you have to take in a few things into mind when it comes to receiving information. Who it is and why they are giving you this information has to be taken into account because some people aren't of good standards when you think they are. Let's just say if it's your girlfriend hasn't had the best of luck with men and has been pressing you to go to the new club. Her motivation for telling what she has told you has to be put into question because a miserable friend will love to see you in the same boat she is in.

But it will be a little different if it's someone who has nothing to gain by revealing information to you. These are the people who genuinely care about your feelings. These are the people you can count on to be by your side regardless of what you go through. These are the people you can learn from. These are people you can grow with.

No matter who it is, their motivations for telling you something that may or may not hurt you has to be put into question. No one just wants to come and tell you something about your relationship when it can have you in pain. Because if most people knew staying out of others' business helps you stay friends a lot longer. In knowing this they wouldn't over-step their boundaries as a friend. I have a saying that was once told to me and I live by it without question and that is, "Believe none of what you hear and half of what you see." I say none of what you hear because even though the information may be good, if you didn't see it for yourself how is it you can say if its true or not. Even when you see something with your own eyes it may not be what it seems.

When you are left to use your imagination about the things, your mind can go in different directions. It holds to be true that you see can sometimes prove to not be what they are and the hard part about that is it's right there in your face and it is not what it seems. So are you going to believe your man or your lying eyes? The problem comes in when others are allowed access into your relationship and more so into your imagination. Sometimes people can mean a world of good but they don't understand the hurt that comes with revealing upsetting information to you. And another thing they don't think of is that the person they are revealing information about no matter the nature of their relationship is that their relationship will change forever by an outside source.

Remember: Your man is old enough to make his own decisions in his life and when he decides to be unfaithful to you this is the decision he has made. He cheated on you and after it comes to light you may do your best to make it work but most of the time it doesn't seem to ever workout once the trust is gone. The worse thing your man can do to you is to betray you and what you have tried to build with him. It's a simple matter you have to make sure you hold him accountable for everything he does and stop making excuses for the things he does wrong. There is never a good reason that I can come up with for being dishonest with the one I say I love. If a man does it, it is something he wants to do and no matter what he says there is nothing he can come up with to cover his unfaithfulness, nothing but the truth. It is not your fault but it is your choice if you decide to stick around and deal with it and you have to know that if he has done it once he may do it again. Regardless of what anyone has to say about the loyalty of your relationship, when cheating is involved there are only two options left. Your options are to stay to try and work it out or to leave.

COMMUNICATION

This is the one way you can assure you have a long-lasting relationship with the one you love. This is the key to the success of not just your relationship but also your life. Communication is the heartbeat of your relationship. I like to say that communication is the constitution of a relationship or go as far as saying it is the holy grail of any relationship. Without it the longevity of whatever you are going through will come and go so fast it will make your head spin. The importance of this aspect of your relationship may be misunderstood simply because you have to understand most men don't really grasp the concept of communication that well. The idea of there being an easy way of communicating should be an easy concept to grasp. But for men it is extremely hard because most men don't know how to open up and tell you what's on their mind and in their hearts. Since guys aren't as open and forthcoming with information about their feelings and don't clearly state what's on there minds, this presents a problem.

Communication is the alpha and omega of any real relationship and I use the term real without hesitation because if you are trying to get something prosperous out of your relationship you have to be able to talk to one an other. When you are trying to build something with a person and you want it to last, you have to be able to open your mouth and say what it is you feel without worrying about the feelings of the person you are having the issue with. Because if there is a problem and you want to address it there is a way to do and say everything in order to get your point across. You have to always keep that in mind because if you don't this opens the door for an argument. You have to take a step back and look at the situation you are about to bring to the table and put yourself in the other person's shoes and think about how you would like to be treated or approach about the issues at hand.

Other than doing this, the argument will stem from how you said what you said and you will lose track of the very reason why you addressed the matter. The why you felt the need to address the issue will go out the window and the flame of how you said what you said will get lit and believe it or not this is how most arguments begin. For example, if you have a problem with some of the females your man has friendship with. Bring this to his attention can be challenging because of a few variables. The nature of their relationship can be an issue. She may just be a friend. Since she is a friend he doesn't think anything is wrong with his socializing with her because it may just be an innocent friendship and you don't know it. Especially if you don't know all of his female friends he grew up with, coworkers, or just friends he has grown to know before he met you. What you have to really understand is some men can have a relationship with a woman that will never end in them having sex. So every female he knows is not a potential sex partner.

The thing to do is to ask him about them in their presence to see how he reacts to the situation. You do this because most men have a tendency to try and avoid most conversations of this nature because they crumble to the pressure. The pressure of having to introduce another female to you with the knowledge you are his girlfriend will put a lot of undo and unpredictable pressure on him and he may crack. Even if she knows about you or just has heard something about you puts him under the gun and he has to be a cold man to pull something off like that without hesitating or giving up the fact he has had a relationship with this woman. The pressure of having two women in the same place at the same time he is sleeping with is hard enough but in the same space and time is unbearable. If its nothing and they are just friends, you will be invited into the conversation like you were there all the time but if it is not don't rush it or put any undo pressure to be let into this world.

The key to knowing where you are in his life is as simple as paying attention to how you are introduced and what he calls you during this process of his introduction. How a man feels about you will show to the world when he brings you into his world. The way he introduces you is very important because the title he gives you lets everyone under the sound of his voice know who you are, he status you have with him and more important than how he wants them to address you as well. If he comes in and introduces you as his girlfriend that lets every woman know he has someone and is not looking and if you are introduced as his wife that lets every woman know he is taken and is obligated to someone. You just have to keep an open mind in the communication aspect of a relationship it can get tricky but it doesn't have to be.

The key to communication is not just talking and getting to know each other, it is also learning to understand each other. If you have someone you can't talk to or are afraid to talk to that relationship won't have a good foundation to grow on and if a man can't talk to you with his mouth he will try different ways of communicating with you. Some of those ways of communicating don't include talking at all. That type of communicating is the reason why some of the relationships turn out like they do and why the statistics of spousal abuse has sky-rocketed. The saying that men can't communicate is a notion developed by women who have gone through countless relationships with men who refused to open up. I say that because there is a way to reach every man you must have an understanding of who that man is.

These are the type of men who have learned sign language but not the traditional language of sign. He has learned to talk with his hands which are mostly balled into fist. Some of the things that women have to endure is not just crazy, it is down right frightening. Some of them have been beaten and broken to the point they believe in their hearts if they don't get beat, the man doesn't love them. They will go through their entire lives with countless numbers of men that abuse them and think that is love. In some cases they will spend their entire lives with this one man who likes for them to look all beat up like something out of a scary movie. I am a firm believer that love is not supposed to hurt in no shape or form in any relationship. I feel if you love someone you can never do anything to hurt them. You will do everything in your power to make sure the only thing you do is to bring happiness into their life. Love is not supposed to burn, bruise, blacken, or knock you out. These are not signs of love, these are forms of hatred and control.

Women have the biggest problem with men because they are open and want for men to be the same way. Men have their own way of dealing with issues in their lives that don't deal with opening the emotional pages of their lives. This comes from how most men are raised. From childhood a boy is taught to be strong and as he grows into a man he is repeatedly told that men don't cry. Even though most men are emotional too they are trained to keep their issues bottled up and that is never good for anyone to do because no one can keep their pain locked away for long.

When dealing with your man sometimes you to deal with him as though he were a child and this isn't a shot at men but understanding that age doesn't determine maturity. When a child acts up you have to find a way to punish that child. For most kids you find what they really like and you take it away from them as a form of punishment. In this instant we are not talking about a child. You have to find ways to get him off of that computer working, get him out of the garage working on his car so he can talk to you. Women have to understand that men are human too and they make mistakes and they fall short sometimes but there has to be some form of communication in order to help the relationship last. After figuring him out you can gain his attention then it is time to discuss whatever it is you have on your mind.

You have to be able to appeal to men just as men have to be able to appeal to you. The communication aspect of a relationship works both ways and even though it seems as if most guys don't have an ear for listening, they do. It takes for it to be something they care about or something that grabs their attention. Not being able to get the special attention they are used to getting is something that men care about. Not being able to drive the nice expensive car they have put so much money into is something men care about. Not being able to lay their head in the same place where they feel absolutely comfortable in is something men care about.

The everyday trials and tribulations are big to most men and they don't put much time or effort into trying to figure out the troubles of the world. If it is not something that affects them directly, men don't care anything about it. Most men are not out to try and save the world and make peace unto all mankind they are just trying to keep everything in their little world in order and nothing else. Because if he does anything else other than what he has already been doing he feels he is trying too hard and will bring himself a lot of undo stress. That's why I say the ability to appeal to men is the key and I am not saying it is to be one-sided but to appeal to men you have to understand the way men think and the important things they care about.

Maybe when you're trying to reach him go at it in a different manner, because during the Sunday's football game is not a good time to talk. Most of you know that and that is why you do it, to spark up an argument just because you know it, but if you want it to work there are some things you just don't do. Date night is a good idea. It gives you time to be alone to talk and it also helps to keep that spark alive in the relationship.

When most men reach the stage in their lives and they consider themselves men they realize it is not about your age but about how you carry yourself as a man. Just because he is thirty-five and he has a nice car he may still have a lot of childish ways he isn't ready to let go of. This is why you will have disagreements when he is thinking one way and you are thinking another. The biggest problem with most men is they don't listen well at all. So when you are trying to reach him on the level he is on you have to make sure you have his undivided attention. Otherwise, you will miss him and he will miss you and that's what you don't want to happen.

Because most disagreements stem from the seed of misunderstanding and the longer it grows the worse off the argument become. How you approach the matter depends on the type of man you are dealing with and the structure of your relationship. That's the reason why I put the most popular types of men in book to help you understand who they are and how to reach them for the reason being each man is different because of who they are. Some men can take the direct approach without a problem and others can't. You have to know who they are first in order to reach them. I use the term man but some men haven't grown to be men and believe me there is a difference.

There is a very wide line between being a man and a boy and a boy's mind-frame can make him think he is a man and he will do everything in his power to convince you and everyone else he is. But a man with a man's standard doesn't need to prove the fact he is a man and he says what he means and means what he says and is able to stand on that word. He lets his actions speak for him and he will not do anything other than what he is use to doing to prove he is the man he is. He will allow you to judge him by his merits and does not have to speak a single word.

The thing is women are left to try and figure out who is who. The hard part about figuring out who is who is because men fake it like a lot of people do. They act as though they are something they are not but they can only act for so long. You have to keep your guard up and try not to fall for anything you are told because the foundation of a relationship is built on trust and stability and without those as a foundation. With the addition of communication, this helps that foundation to stand the test of time. It is easy to get caught up in the games men play because woman have a desire for the situation to work. You do your best to make it last. It will not last when you're dealing with certain types of men your best efforts still won't be good enough because of the breakdown in communication. Someone's antenna isn't up to receive the signal or you may just be on the wrong frequency but you have to work on it in order for it to work like you want it to.

It's a simple process but it is difficult to implement into a relationship at times because you have to try and get on the same page and in the same frame of mind. You have to be able to put all your foolish pride aside and allow the relationship to grow and blossom. You have to think of your relationship as you would a flower. It starts off as a seed but only in the proper conditions will it grow into a beautiful flower that is so appealing to the eye. Thus; communication is the water to the flower and as a flower needs the water, a relationship needs the watering of communication to survive. Communication is needed from the first to the last day of a relationship. Even though the flower is planted it will still need the necessary nutrients and care in order to grow to its full potential and the same is for your relationships. They both need all of the necessary ingredients to work.

One approach is the direct approach. It has its advantages and disadvantages as does any other method of approach. This one helps to make sure your point gets across in a hurry. This approach for some men is difficult to deal with from women because it seems as though you are attempting to test their manhood but it's not intended to go across like that even though sometimes it does. So you have to know your man, how his character is, and if he is able to handle you being so straight to the point on some of those important issues.

Again the objective of it all is to reach him so he can understand the point you are trying to get across to him. To challenge a man is the last thing you really want to do because it puts him on the defense and as long as his defensive walls are up it makes it just that much more difficult to talk to him. This method works to get your point across but it sometimes causes more confusion than is really needed, depending on your delivery. That's when a simple quiet conversation can turn into a yelling match and that's not what you want. For those men who can't take the direct approach you have to be a little mindful when this approach is implemented. This woman has really gotten tired of some of the things you have been putting out. So you can say this approach is sometimes used out of the frustrations in the relationship. The thing with this approach is there will be no misunderstandings about what you're trying to say and even though it may end up in a little bit of yelling but it may do the job if he doesn't turn a deaf ear to the yelling.

Other approaches are a little more subtle. They help to get your point across to the person you are attempting to reach. They work also but they are not as direct. No matter the form of communication you are attempting to use, at least you are trying. I know it is a difficult task to do because you never know where his head is at but if you keep trying you will get it right. It's more about getting to know your man or should I say learning him just as he should get to know you. In the process of learning him, you will learn how to talk to him and deal with him on the level you have to communicate with him on. I like to call this the growing process in which you will learn about the man you are dealing with and you learn to grow with who he is and he grows learn you and when you can grow together it turns out to be a beautiful thing. It is at this point when you grow as a couple and people can look at what you have become and become a little envious of what you have.

The process is not a hard one but can be a timely one depending on the type of man you have come in contact with it. The deeper his mind is and the more values he has, the longer it may take for him to open up. The stronger he is the harder it is to break down some of those barriers he has in place. In letting you in, the defensive walls he has up will come down without any difficulty and this will allow you to help groom your relationship into what you both want it to be. Even though he may be a strong individual with a high value system when it is all said and done he is still a man and he desires to have someone who compliments him by his side. He still breathes like any other man. He still feels pain, happiness or sorrow just like any other man.

The process can be a difficult one but it is a necessary one to go through. The walls you break through will help the relationship go a lot smoother than you could ever have imagined. The conversations will be more pleasant and instead of arguing you will be able to sit and talk and have a quiet meaningful conversation about whatever it is that either of you have on your mind. This way you can ensure you will be able to get your point across and he will be able to enlighten you on his point of view on the matter at hand. The yelling and the arguing will be things of the past. The door for growth in your relationship will open for you and the gentleman you are with. After this point, it will be more about listening more so than listening so you can respond. When you are able to let go and understand that in a relationship it is about both of you. Meaning anyone outside of the relationship and whatever opinions they have they can keep them to themselves.

The things that are important to men they will fight, claw and even die for. But when a man finds something to live for that is greater than anything. This is why men sometimes look over the small things women find near and dear to them. We are not that much different from each other, we just have different views. This is why we have to be able to open up and discuss the issues of our life so we can get to the bottom of our problems but also to learn more of the person we are pairing ourselves off with. We talk to inform each other on how we feel about the issues of our live, the things we like, the things we love or just the day to day issues that may come up. The better we understand how and why we feel the way we feel. The better we understand the person we are with and why they do what they do. One of the reasons why we do so is to help us get a better understanding of the mindset of the person you are spending your time with. So the time you are spending won't be a waste of time and it will be meaningful and prosperous.

At times our views about situations in our lives can get obstructed. Sometimes it is our pride or maybe it is just our will for things not to be true is what drives us. No matter the issue that any couple may face it is always good to have an open line of communication. This way there are no surprises and there are no obstacles they cant face together. I keep stating the obvious but communication is the key to any working relationship. It can be your job relationship or a relationship between siblings no matter the nature of the relationship communication is key.

Remember: When you are in a relationship you have to keep a line of communication open in order to make sure everyone is on the same page. When you learn to communicate with your mate you make it easier for the relationship to work. When you talk with your mate, they will be able to come to you with anything and when you can talk through the problems that may present themselves most things will get worked out. The problems develop in most relationships come in when two people can't come into an agreement about an issue in their relationship. This is only a problem for the couples who can't seem to see things eye to eye. Couples who have been together for a while have learned each other. They know that no matter what happens their better half will be there for them. They have also learned to us communication as a gateway to compromise and it leads to everyone having a clear understanding of each others mindset.

PLACEMENT

This is one of the important things to remember in a relationship and the difficult part about this is most people don't understand where their place is in their relationship. It's hard in most relationships because most people don't talk about where they are held in the relationship and this is the reason why I included this as one of the chapters. If more people are open to discuss the real nature of the relationship, this wouldn't be a problem but most men will lie and deceive the women in their lives to keep them on a leash in order to keep them around.

The trouble with this is sometimes we have a way of taking things people tell us to heart because our hearts lead us to want to be loved and want to believe we are loved. Even though at times we know it will not last, we put our trust in the words that are said. In doing this, the placement of who we are or what we are to the person we are in the relationship with is thrown off track. Just because someone says they love you doesn't mean they are reciprocating the same love to you or understand the love you have for them. In dealing with most men, playing the emotional card could be a ploy to keep you around because there is something you have or something you are giving that they like which pushes them to keep you around. They will play on your emotions for as long as you allow. It happens on both sides of the ball, both men and women alike have this problem with the deception and this is the main reason the placement gets thrown off in a relationship.

The placement process is a very simple one because all you have to do is be honest with the one you are with. You have to know it will be made difficult when the honesty isn't there and when you have a key aspects of a relationship missing, there will always be problems. Although if the honesty is there in the relationship a relationship can be one of those that will be strong and will last for as long as you do. There used to be a time when the placement was already understood in a relationship and in the family. There used to be a time when it was possible to fall in love and have a family and watch your kids and grand kids grow into adults in peace but that time is one of the past.

Do you remember the times when granddaddy and grandmother got along just fine, simply because the both knew their roles inside of their relationship? Even though those were a more simple time, the relationship structure was still the same and the growth process of the relationship itself was still the same. Granddaddy was the provider. He did most of the work that dealt with putting food on the table and keeping the bills paid, not because he had to but because it was the responsible thing for him as a man to do. He was the man of the house and what he said was law inside of the walls of his home. Grandmother was his backbone. In some cases she was the house wife and she did all the necessary things around the house to make sure he didn't have to do much when he got home from those long hard days of work. It wasn't because he made her do it, but it was necessary to keep the affairs of the house and the family in order. She did what it took to make sure the house ran in an orderly fashion and everyone in the house knew she was the second-in-command and didn't question the law of the house.

Even though granddaddy was the money-maker of the family, he would turn the money over to grandmother and she took care of the bills and kept the refrigerator and the pantry filled with food that fed the family and anyone else who came knocking. Its not like granddaddy couldn't do those things he just didn't have to because he had the necessary help it took to keep the family functioning properly. He didn't have to argue and fight with his wife because she and he knew what it took to make a relationship work for thirty-five years. They had structure or placement as I like to call it well put together. They didn't argue much and if they did the kids didn't hear much of it and they kept them out of the hardships of the family until the children were old enough to understand.

If there were problems in the house, it was almost never seen or heard of because they knew everything had its time and its place for discussion. The placement was almost never broken and everything stayed within the guidelines of the placement. It was never spoken but always understood. Regardless of what any one says, understanding is the best thing in the world. The understanding of how someone feels about you. When you don't have to take a guess at what is meant by another person's actions this helps you to deal with the issues that will come about.

The thing about placement is that it takes the guess work out of the process. There will be no reason to second guess why certain things are happening in the relationship. If he buys you something he is doing it out of the kindness of his heart and doesn't have any other agenda behind it. If he does for you like no other man has, it's because he feels you have done enough to deserve it and have earned it and even more. When he feels the world is what you are worth, even though he may not be able to give it to you, in his dreams that is exactly what he sees. You having everything, being able to go where ever you wish and enjoying the world with him. When it gets anywhere near this point the placement of the relationship has to be discussed and the discussion has to go deeper than any other conversation you have ever had. This is one of those times when the values, the potential, or just the whole moral fiber of your relationship has to be brought into the forefront. This very important discussion is the ground in which your relationship will be built on from that day forth.

The placement of who you are and where you stand in your relationship doesn't happen over night. It is not just given away, and even the strong have to learn to be submissive at times if they want to keep the love they have in their lives. It has been said the best leaders are those who learned how to follow first. It is not enough to be the man or the dominant driving force in the relationship. For a man to be able to lead the relationship he has to know how to be the man of the relationship.

It isn't enough to be the driving force of a relationship if you don't know where to drive the relationship. This is one of the issues facing the relationships of this day and age. Most women want a dominant man or an alpha male in their lives that will help steer their relationship into the right direction but they are not willing to allow someone to take the driver's seat. The thing about being in the driver's seat you have to know the seat can be adjusted to fit any driver that is able to drive and that means man or woman. The circumstances of the relationship process has changed into something that makes it difficult to see how this is supposed to be at times.

Let's say you are a thirty-five-year-old female and you are in a relationship and you decide to reenter into college and finish what you started about finishing your degree because you had a child and couldn't finish. If you have the right type of man leading you in the right direction, he will carry the load for you as long as it takes. When you get into school if necessary he would pick up another job and probably help you with your homework if there is something he can help you with. He will do this the right way and for the right reasons. He will help you grow into the person you want to grow into because he loves you and wants you to be the best you that you can be. This helps to build up the placement of the relationship because no matter how you look at it, when one person in the relationship prospers the whole family prospers too. When the relationship grows the love grows. It's not just your graduation it is the whole family's degree of success. If you think about it no one can do anything by themselves. We all need some type of support but when you have the right support things seem to go so much better. This works for all life-altering situations that may present themselves. If you don't have the right man to be there to help and is willing to be there for you, those things will be more difficult. This goes for when you want to relocate to another city. He will be there to get things situated first before sending for you. You may have an idea of changing careers. He sees the good and the bad of the change but he will be there for you and no matter what it is he will do his best to support you through all you do.

What really gets the ball rolling the right way is a man with the right plan that is capable of leading you and himself in the appropriate direction the proper way. This may be one of the more prosperous and fulfilling ways that could be a little more demanding but when you finally get there it will be well worth the wait. No matter what people say when you are in a good relationship the food you eat seems to taste better. You see the thing that comes along with this is what some women have a problem with and that is being submissive without fault. If he is a good man, you have to be able to let go of whatever it is in your mind is causing you to hesitate to live your life and enjoy some of life's pleasures.

Sometimes the plan we have for ourselves is not what is in our life cards but we still have to play the hand that is dealt to us to the fullest of our abilities. When you can set aside all the distrust, the skepticism, or even your past that has held you back for so long, you can learn to live and enjoy your life. The submissiveness comes in when you can learn to trust the man you are with to do right by you. It doesn't come easy and it takes the trials you face to get to this point in order to really see the foundation your relationship is built on. I know its not an easy road to travel but it has to be traveled in order to get to where you want to be. Even though nothing is really promised to us except for the fact we will live and die but love is something that has to be earned and worked on continuously and when you finally get it, it has to be cherished and nurtured.

Placement works both ways. The rules apply for women as well as it does for men. Depending on what type of guy it is you are dealing with, depends on the type of relationship and the type of placement that you have. All men are men but all men are not as headstrong and as dependable as my granddaddy was. Just as all women aren't as mindful and as submissive as my grandmother was. That is why you have to know who you are with, so you will be able to determine how your relationship will be structured. That's one of the things we have to remember because a lot of people have a habit of comparing their relationship with others and that is unfair to your mate.

No two relationships are exactly the same just like no two people are exactly the same. No matter how much you want your relationship to be, it will never be like another person's relationship. You have to be willing to make the necessary changes within yourself to make sure it gets to where you want it to be. Because you don't have a clue what they went through and the sacrifices they to make to get their relationship to where it is, there is no way you can ever compare the two. The game will never be the same simply because the players in the game are not the same and the circumstances are not either. That's why you can't hope for what someone else has in their relationship, unless its happiness.

When you know who you are and what you are truly worth the understanding of each situation is handled a lot better. When you know who you are, there are doors to meet people and allow them to come in to your world. If you let them, they will grow to be some of the best friends you will ever have. When you know your value there are things that come about in life you will not settle for and sometimes settling for less is the reason why you end up in some of the situations you are currently in.

As you come across the people in your everyday life, you will be able to determine who is and who isn't worthy of being friends with but that is only if you are paying attention to the things people do. If you are not paying attention you will miss something important attributes about them. It may be something you may not like. It's not that you're better than anyone else but when people meet their attitudes have to be compatible with one another in order to be able to bond. One conversation with a person should let you know if they are to be or not to be someone who you can look upon as a friend.

Just take this in perspective for a second. Let's say you're starting a new job and you are getting acquainted with the people in the office and in the process you have some alone time with each individual there over a period of time. There is going to be someone you're not going to see eye to eye with and it's not you it's them. After you get the manner in how you should deal with them, you will know how to treat them. It's not like you went into the office to single them out from everyone else but there will be a little conflict because your attitudes will clash. This is the same way you have to deal with people in your personal life, just in a different fashion. Everything and everyone has their place in your life but it's up to you to figure out how to deal with them.

This placement I speak of varies from relationship to relationship and it also changes with the growth of the relationship. As the relationship grows so does the responsibility of the individuals in the circle of the relationship so when that happens it has to be a mutual understanding between both parties. There is a difference in the relationship when you're living the single life and you and your significant other don't live under the same roof. The rules of engagement within the relationship are different from that of a committed one. There are things that you don't have to answer for and you can come and go as you please without having your actions questioned by anyone.

I really do admire my grandparent's relationship. I know it didn't get like that over night and there was plenty of hard work put in for it to get to that point. We all have to remember it had to start somewhere. There had to be some type of foundation laid out in order for me to see the beauty in their relationship as it was. The transition from being single and doing as you wish and having to be considerate about the feelings of another is a really deep process for men.

This is made difficult for a number of reasons but I feel the number one reason for the misunderstanding is things aren't properly discussed. The real trouble with the misunderstanding is men think they can still do the things they used to do like they used to do them but they can't because there is a level of respect that you have to have for the person he is with. Most men are so head strong it is crazy. Men have to learn to be more caring when it comes to their women and their feelings. Some don't grasp the concept of thinking for someone else or being considerate enough to put themselves in the shoes of another. If men could do that without having to go through so many unnecessary trials of trying to find out who they are, the world would be so much better. When you can sit back and discuss issues in the relationship, there is a level of understanding that is built. He learns you don't like for him to have four o'clock mornings that don't include you or without letting you know it will be one of those nights. Something as simple as a phone call to inform you he will be out there is something simple to do but is doesn't get done all the time. But ladies, you have to understand those things you feel are simple are not so to men because those things have to be learned and practiced. Or should I say it has to be taught by you because when you open your mouth to let him know it bothers you, he should try to do better to help save face on the relationship and this shows you he is compassionate about your feelings.

That is how the placement of your relationship is built through the dos and don'ts of the relationship. No man should go through a relationship with a woman if he intends on hurting her but you have men out here that don't care about your feelings. That's why you have to go through the proper phases with the men in order to be able to determine what their motives are. I am disappointed you have to go through this with some of the men you encounter but it is needed in order for you to be able to allow your heart to feel love. That love you acquire during this time is what I like to call concentrated love because of the fact it helps to strengthen that relationship. It focuses on doing the small things which helps the bond between you and your mate grow stronger. The strength comes in to play when you don't have to question him anymore and you get to the point to where you can trust in him to do what he needs to do. There is no second guessing his every move. That concentrated love is the reason why people say you have a glow about you and they notice you are happy with what you have in your life. Rather than worrying about the small things in life, you can concentrate on more important issues of your life, like your future.

It may seem like a bother to have to go through the same things with just about every man you come in contact with but it is absolutely necessary in order to build the relationship you wish to have. You can never do enough to test a man to make sure he is the man you want in your life. You have to make sure he has the will to do what it takes to get you and keep you happy while he has you and you have to have the same desire. Some men will respond well to you trying to get a feel for who he is but some of the men will not. But it is your choice in the matter if you continue to try and build something with this type of man who will not make you happy.

Remember: If you feel he is not the one for you, nine times out of ten he isn't and there will be nothing you will be able to do to change that. There is no changing some men they will forever be who they are. But if you have someone good and genuine who loves you unconditionally and it feels good, do what you can to make sure it works because happiness is harder to find than the leprechaun's pot of gold at the end of a rainbow. When you finally find someone who is what you want it is going to be a bumpy ride because just as you have obstacles in your life he is going to have some too. However; if you can learn to grow together and help each other weather through the storm, you will learn to enjoy the beautiful sunny days together. And please keep this in mind, there is not going to be this storybook ending that some people look for.

BREAK UPS

This is one of the most difficult parts of any relationship. No matter how anyone thinks, if you love someone the last thing you want to do is to see them walk out of your life. Most have been there and there are some breakups that end okay but that rarely happens. The bad thing about a break up is we feel we really loved this person we have grown to know and it is unimaginable to go on with our lives without them. But when it gets to the point when you want to leave or your significant other has decided to leave you something has happened that has caused this to happen. There is something someone has missed, there is something you didn't do or the person has simply just gotten tired of dealing with you and the baggage you have brought into the relationship. Most men get bored more easily than women and with this boredom there come a number of problems.

The bad thing about a breakup, it seems to come at the worst times of a relationship. No matter how much you think you are, no one is really ready for a situation like this. Sometimes breakups happen so suddenly because something dramatic has happened that forces the situation to come about. For instance, if someone is caught cheating and the other half doesn't want to work it out. The relationship is over and there is nothing to be done or said to improve the matter. I like to call these types of breakups the combustible ones because at any given time, depending on the actions that take place, the entire relationship will blow up in your face. Whatever the reason for the implosion or explosion of the relationship the outcome is never pretty and will turn uglier the longer you try and drag things out.

The weird thing about even the most combustible situations we still try and work them out no matter how bad the problem has gotten because at this point we are thinking with our hearts. Sometimes in relationships we have to learn to let live and let go because the longer we try and hold on, the longer we suffer through the troublesome problems. No matter how strong you are or claim to be, to lose someone you care for hurts. It is easier to say than do at times but we have to be strong enough to let go. You try to hold on for as long as we can because no one wants to deal with those lonely days and nights alone. One of the worse things to deal with after a breakup is that lonely feeling of just being alone. Those nights that start with a bottle of wine and end with ice cream and a sad movie and a face full of tears.

This is the time when you try and find something to replace whatever the void is you have lost in your relationship. The cruel and unusual thing about this situation is you try to compensate for what you have lost. You try to fill the void with things that don't suit you but you do them anyway. Those long nights of bar-hopping when you vaguely remember how you got home or with whom you got home with. Or maybe those unforgettable times you had with your friends checking out the new clubs that end up in you meeting guy after guy who only remind you of the low-down, no good guy who you just had to leave and ending your nights just reminiscing over him again.

The time you really need is some time to yourself to regroup to see what direction you are going to go in. The difficult part about being lonely is you have to really take the time to think rationally about the next step you're going to make. If you took the time to think, you would realize the one person you should always love is you. That's the kind of thing we need to be reminded of during those times when we have these feelings of worthlessness or hopelessness.

You have to try and realize no matter how bad you feel there are better days headed your way and, if you are patient, those days will be so much more enjoyable. In this time, you will have hours to figure out who you are and who you want to become. In time you will eventually find someone but during this time you should find yourself. You just have to give yourself time to breathe a little to clear your mind. When you finally get things together you may be surprised who the new person will be in your life. That unsuspecting person you would have never looked at in this manner if you had never gone through that untimely break up. The best person for you may be standing right next to you. They have your best interests at heart and by them already seeing you have been hurt they don't want to see you go through that anymore.

WHY ASK WHY? WHEN YOU SAY WE'RE STUPID ANYWAY | 119

But it is different for men on the level of a breakup because the majority of the time, they are the cause of the problem. They try and do everything in there power to make up for the mistakes they made. The hard part about any breakup especially from a man's point of view is seeing the woman he loves with another man. It hurts even worse when she is getting treated better and seems to be happier. To see you down and out, looking like you are suffering without him, or just haven't been able to completely get over him is what men like to see and that is what they prey on.

You have to try and be able to look at it from a man's stand point. Let's just say it has been eight months or so after the breakup and the phone calls have stopped and you see him out and even though he has done wrong by you, he convinces you that he has changed and you fall for it. This is one of the ways that men will prey on you because you want to believe so much in your heart he has changed and is a better person. The only thing he has gotten better at is being able to deceive you and the only thing he misses is the sex. In a more simple term, he has found a better way to get away with lying and cheating.

When you split up and back track there was a reason for that but no matter how forgiving your heart is you have to try to stick to your guns. I will tell you like my grandmother used to tell me, "Life lessons are just that, lessons and with lessons you have to pay the price for them and it may cost you a little or it may cost you a lot but it will cost you." When you say goodbye you have to keep pressing on in order to make sure you have a steady head because if you don't you will set yourself up for unnecessary headaches. When he wants to get back into a relationship with you its mainly because he is missing something that you have to offer him.

The real problem with taking someone back is it's not like starting a new relationship because this person already knows you. They know what it takes to please you and knows what it takes to get to your heart. The problem comes with this "taking someone back" is you can never know if what they say is actually the truth or even if they are being sincere. You have to know this is not a new flame. It is an old one and an old flame has all the necessary tools to get to the center of you. This old flame of yours knows what to say and knows what to do. They know how to keep your mind occupied because this flame has figured out how to get better at trickery and deception. There are the occasions where they are real about what they say and mean because in your absence they may have realized what they lost and want it back.

It's not a bad idea to try and find some good in someone who has caused you a little grief in the past but I still feel it is not a good idea to back track unless you are 100% sure. The relationship process can be a very difficult one but it can still be a very adventurous one depending on your outlook on life. The thing about it all is when you have entered a relationship you want the person you are with to be real and honest with you. But when you reenter a relationship with someone you have a history with it doesn't open up new doors but reopens up more painful old ones you may have wanted to forget. You may have forgiven them but you haven't forgotten anything.

Those memories are still planted in your mind and after the first argument you have those memories will soon surface. Please remember this, "Some people are meant to be in your life for a season and some people are meant to be in your life for a lifetime and you have to be able to determine who those people are."

Dating someone from your past brings about the reason why you left them and remember in life you have to keep going and moving on in order to flourish. Your future is not in your past but your future is determined by your past because of the trials that life takes you through. These trials help to determine who you are. We all can sometimes be a little passive and would like to believe people can learn to be better people as time goes on. But people learn to adapt and evolve into smarter and more conniving individuals that have developed a talent of doing better work. Deep in our hearts we want to believe they have learned from their past mistakes. Without the belief someone can change it would be difficult for anyone to get beyond the first level of your defenses.

This belief will enable you from the rational thinking you normally do to get through situations on a day to day basis. The anticipation of wanting it to happen is worse than actually finding out it's a lie. Because you want to believe in it you want for it to be as good as you hope it to be but in the end it's not and you can't blame anyone but yourself. Because you set yourself up for failure. It's kind of like being a kid and you have done something and got in trouble for it. You know you're going to get a whooping for it but the anticipation of the whooping was actually worse than the whooping itself.

And that's like hoping for someone to be something that are not, you can feel it in the pit of your stomach things aren't right but you put your instincts on hold just to put unnecessary obstacles in your own way and in the process you your own build stumbling blocks. Sometimes you have to pay attention to the gut feelings you have about certain circumstances you go through because you normally are right with your assumptions but you have to learn. At times you have to be mindful of the sensations you have about many of the issues of the time. That feeling pays off most of the time. I don't look at it as a man's or a woman's thing, because we all have it we just have different reactions to it.

Some people, like myself, use this feeling as a way to see things before they come. That uneasy feeling lets me know to back away from the situation and take a deeper look to see if I would really want to make another mistake and get my feelings involved in this particular matter. My open mind, in combination with the time I take to evaluate the matter, seems to help me come to a good decision that works out in my favor. The last thing I want is for me is to be hurt again and the pain that comes along with that is one that no man or woman wants to feel on a regular basis. Especially by someone who has done it to you before. In doing it like this, I have to have developed the patience and a presence of mind to make myself aware of the obstacles that may present themselves.

You don't have to be able to be a psychic in order to foresee a mistake in the making. The beautiful part of doing this is you save yourself a lot of heartache and pain thus making you a better person for the next essential relationship you have. For this reason you will not make the same mistake you made with the previous relationship and if you see the trend you set going in the wrong direction you can rectify the matter before it gets worse. In doing so, you can reassure yourself if it is possible to work things out you can. The difficult part of doing this is when you see it coming the other party may not understand your actions. Your significant other may not understand why you are doing what you are doing. They may not realize why you are distancing yourself from them. So be ready to do a little explaining in order to help the relationship work out. Because when you're doing things in your relationship and others don't understand there will be a number of questions that will be asked. So you have to look at it as in it being a gift and a curse at the same time.

Then you have those that don't pay any attention to this feeling and just go through their lives trying to make it and have trouble doing so mainly because they have trouble with the vision of their third eye. Occasionally, its when you can see things that are to come and can see them unfold but some people will ignore the signs on the wall and keep going the route they are taking and get hurt until they can finally see for themselves. But the problem with that is when you're just winging it you end up with a lot of unwanted pains that come along with the mistakes. You have to realize if something doesn't feel right, it isn't and you have to learn to walk away from things in your life that aren't right. However when you look past errors people make and make up excuses for them, you are settling and don't even know it. When you settle you sell yourself short and will miss out on some of the real pleasures of life. One of the pleasures that I can assure you will miss out on is happiness and for most people, happiness is the first pleasure they strive for. On the other hand when you can't see what your happiness is or you just don't know what it is that makes you happy, sadness is what you find. The solution is a very simple one and you have to be able to find yourself first but when you don't know exactly what it is you are looking for inside of you no one can make you happy. You have to be able to make you happy first. But when you are walking blind into relationships with people there will be a little pain involved.

Most people get a little traumatized by losing someone they love and you have good reason to because of the emotional attachments you have with that person. Like I have heard people say, "Everything gets better in time." This is true but who wants to spend time hurting. The process alone is one that happens but sometimes you have to look at situations in a different manner. Maybe you had to lose that person you were with in order to get someone who is more suitable for you. Sometimes it is a good thing to have to go through situations of that nature because it opens your eyes to see life through a better lens.

Occasionally when dealing with situations of this magnitude, you have to be able to live and learn because that pain comes with a lesson. You are supposed to learn something about yourself out of every experience you go through. The lessons you learn are supposed to take you a little further along in your life to make you a better person. When you have to continue to go through the same situations with different people, at some point you have to realize it is not them, it is you. One of the hardest things people have to experience is having to find fault inside of themselves. No one likes to take the time to do a little soul searching and taking a real look in the mirror. Can you imagine taking the time to study who you are and repair you and who you are, and do self-evaluations of yourself or like I sometimes say a self-overhaul? I know that it is easy to say but hard to do but periodically we need to stop looking for the downfalls in others and check ourselves first no matter how difficult it may be.

With the hurt, I have learned, men and women deal with it in different ways and sometimes with men it doesn't make them a better person to deal with because men don't know how to let go sometimes. Most guys can remember their first love and how the relationship ended. You are thirty-two and you find yourself comparing your current girlfriend with your high school sweetheart. This is a problem. A problem simply because it shows he still haven't moved on from his first love situation. The growing up process includes maturing and moving on. When you bring baggage into a relationship you also bring in problems and that is what most guys do and don't even know it. What most men have a difficulty in understanding that women all share some of the same characteristics simply because they are women and you can't compare one with the other because even though women are similar they still are just that much different. When guys do this, it shows that even though they think they are ready to be in a committed relationship they are not and will only bring confusion into the relationship. Guys don't have any idea they are carrying this baggage.

Here comes the problem when he meets you and you are a loving and caring person, are willing to look past some of his short comings, and he doesn't appreciate you. We as men have a serious problem with letting go. I don't know if it is a part of our DNA or if it has something to do with our pride but letting go is difficult for us. Guys will hold on to you and cling to you for as long as you allow them to. That's why most men are pack rats and have a bunch of useless things they will never use again but will find a place for it to collect dust. The same goes for relationships as well. If you don't make a real effort to let some guys know it is over he will continue to act as though the relationship still exists. And sometimes when you do make the necessary moves to let him know it is over he still may not get the picture.

Take this into consideration the next time you find yourself in a situation where you are about to break up with your man. Doing it over the phone, texting, or leaving a message is not the answer. A man needs to be able to look you in the eyes to see you are serious about what it is you are trying to get across to him. Because the love he thinks he has for you may not allow him to take you serious.

No man really understands it is over unless he has done something wrong to cause you to leave him. It doesn't set in that he has done things over time and you have gotten fed up with it and that's why you have to make up your mind to leave him. At this point, he wants to talk but you are already talked out. You have made up your mind already and there is nothing he can do to make you change your mind.

This is the point where he is going to do everything that he can to show you he has changed and is willing to change to see if he can get you to have a change of heart. He is doing this because he knows he was wrong and he will do and say anything to try and right those wrongs now. Remember, this is only temporary. He is doing this now to try and salvage the relationship. The trouble with this strategy is most men can only hold on to the changes for a while and will revert back to their old ways. If he was doing so because it was something he wanted to do while you were together, this would be great for your relationship. This is only temporary. It probably will never occur to him if he put forth a fraction of the effort during the relationship these problems you are having wouldn't be so bad. But because he procrastinated and dismissed your needs this is why things have gotten so far out of hand.

When it gets like this the flowers show up on your job, he welcomes you home with open arms, or he begins to takes you out. All of this is so far out of his character you can see it has no substance, none at all. But your emotional side will kick in and you will allow him to come back in and believe me once he has made his way back in he will fall back into his old ways. The truth of the matter is and I may reiterate this fact a number of times in this writing no matter how far your relationship goes, no matter the twists and turns it may take you as a woman have total control over the relationship.

The reason I say this is because men go out their way to do things to make an impression on women and women can dictate the outcome of any situation that may develop in a relationship. The way things go is funny because everything has its natural order and when the order is followed everything seems to flow better. Men have their way of thinking but women have a slight upper hand when dealing with relationships and sometimes women have a tendency to forget this fact. You have to remember no matter what has happened you will be all right and sooner or later someone will come along to fill that void in your heart but you just can't settle for just anything. You have to know we are all human and in being human there are always places for error because we are not perfect.

Remember: When the relationship has reached its end there is no turning back and there is no working it out. Whatever the reason is you have decided or he has decided to part ways with you, it is over and life goes on and you have to be ready for something bigger and better to come into your life. Even though it is over, you have to be able to recognize your life goes on and even though it may hurt to see him leave maybe that is the best thing for you. So when the time comes do something you enjoy so that you can get back on your feet and start enjoying life again.

COMPATIBILITY

When dealing with the men in your life, the hardest part is finding someone you can be truly happy with, or should I say someone you are compatible with. This is one of the keys that will help you to find happiness in your life. With compatibility you can reassure yourself the person you are with is one of the people you can depend on to be there for you and will keep your best interests in mind and in heart. This man will be one of those men you can find a world of happiness in because you will find all the things in a man you desire. He will be there for you doing the things you like to do, not because he feels obligated to do so but because it makes you happy and seeing you happy.

This aspect of the relationship is why you see the couple that everyone wants to be like and this is the reason why they will always have an admirable relationship. They have learned what it takes to make each other happy and that is what it is really about. Being able to put aside your wants and putting someone before yourself is one of those special traits many people don't have. This is the part of the relationship in which the man you are with will put all of his selfishness aside and make sure that every day he can look you in your eyes and make you smile without saying a word.

It doesn't always work out like this and if it did there wouldn't be any need for this book or any other of its kind. But for this imperfect world we live in let me get down to the surface of things and dig a little deeper to open up everyone's eyes. You see the key part of compatibility is being able to compromise and with compromise there come a lot of problems for most men. With compromising there brings along the idea of men having to give up some of the things they enjoy and giving up time they are not used to giving up. This is the point when you can tell if your man is sincere about the things he speaks of because if he loves you like he claims there shouldn't be a problem.

Compromise is a word that most men care not to speak and wouldn't care to ever know the definition of simply because they like things their way and they will stand on it as long as you as a woman allow them to. It has been said men are pig-headed and headstrong and want for everything to go their way. Most men are just as you think they are and are a lot more selfish than you can ever imagine and would like for things to go their way but you as the woman have the power to change all he knows. What I mean is ladies you make all types of changes to try and make your relationship work with your man and why shouldn't he make some of the same changes or compromises you make. You do it out of the kindness of your heart to make sure you're doing your part in the relationship and why shouldn't he? He doesn't do that because he doesn't feel he has to. Most men have a tendency to think of themselves as kings but what they don't understand is as a king you have to be able to carry thyself as a king and lead as a king does. Most men don't have these qualities in them to even compare themselves as a king but they do but lack the qualifications. This is one of the factors that make it hard for them to be able to compromise with the women in their lives. Eventually they will learn to do so after so many ups and downs in their relationships. They will learn to cater to their woman in ways that will make their woman happy without compromising any of the attributes that make him a man.

Women you have to push the button on this issue because if you don't he will think everything is fine and think you are satisfied with the man he is even when you're not. So you have to press the issue in a cunning and slick way that he doesn't even realize he is even being pushed. When a man thinks he is winning it is easy to manipulate his mind and body into doing whatever it is you want him to do. There isn't anything hard about it because if you are a woman and you are used to having your way, you already know what it takes to make this happen.

The only thing that you have to remember is that most men don't process information as fast as they think and they leave themselves open for situations like this. The situations of mind play and a little deception to get what it is you want. It's not that you are lying it's just you are doing what it takes to get what you want out of your man. It may get a little confusing to him at times because your actions will have him trying to figure out whats going on. But when he gets to the point of understanding his woman better you both begin to win.

But the compatibility comes in to play when he is doing what it is you wish of him to do to keep you happy and you are doing what it is he wants of you. If you were a little flirtatious when you first met him and you changed your ways to accommodate him, this is what I mean. When you are in the relationship you will make the necessary changes within yourself in order to make sure that relationship works but some men need extra help in order to get there. Most men are so hard-headed they can know what it takes to make you happy but they let their egos get in the way of just doing the right thing. The right thing being to make sure he does what he needs to do to make you happy and satisfy all of your needs. When his pigheadedness gets in the way, it makes it difficult for him to keep a proper perspective on what it takes to do this. He has to learn you and how you think, your likes, and your dislikes. There has to be something set in place with your man to help him understand what it takes to make you get to the climax of your day.

You see compatibility is the will of getting to know the likes just as well as the dislikes and being able to make theirs yours. Men have to be able to see into you, in order to make things work between you two. It almost has to be like a spiritual awakening of some sort. He has to learn to read your mind and your body to make this happen.

I like the taste of cheese but I can't eat it. So when my sweetheart cooks she thinks of me and instead of that side of macaroni and cheese she will make an additional side dish that I can eat to satisfy my hunger. Its not hard to do or something you have to go well out of your way to make the other person happy. It helps the relationship grow when you have the other person in mind when you do whatever you do. The reason why she does this is because she loves me but she also does it because she knows I have to be selective about what I eat. In return she is rewarded with a kiss and that is not just any kiss it is one of thanks and it let her know that I appreciate everything she does even when she doesn't have to.

In a relationship, you may have to do a number of things you don't necessarily like or care much for but to keep down on the confusion you will do so. You may have a man and he is a real sports fanatic. You may not care for sports much but you will take the time to learn something about the sports and the teams he enjoys watching. This is the point when your compassion for him helps you to put aside your likes for a while to make sure you know something about his likes to help things go a little easier. It's not that you are trying to overstep your boundaries or anything. This helps out on conversations or just to be able to get into a conversations that may take place about the sport.

The beauty of this is the more you can participate in the actions of his life the more you will learn about him and the doors for more will open. In the process you will break down some of those barriers he has up. It is always good to be able to talk and interact with people on their level because it makes it easier to deal with each other. It's a lot easier to talk about sports with your man when you actually know something about the sport topic that is at hand. It doesn't just have to be about sports, it is just easier to speak on topics you have some knowledge about.

This becomes a problem for men because society has grown to know the tough and rugged men who are hard and gritty. Everyone likes that old Clint Eastwood type of man but every man can't be that guy. There has to be more to a man than just an outlook or a character; there has to be more substance. Since every man can't be that strong and tough there has to be men out there that live their everyday lives and will cry and show their emotional side. Have you ever looked at that gentleman in the store holding his wife's purse while she tries on a dress? You know good well he doesn't want to be there holding that purse but it is shopping day and he will hold that bag for hours if need be to keep her happy.

This is the thing that most people find it difficult to understand because of the way the man has been portrayed in the past. The man is supposed to be strong and is supposed to be this tough individual but things get a little deeper. Men cry too. If they show this in public like women do they are sometimes looked upon as being weak or even as far as being soft. It just varies on the individual and their strengths and weaknesses because in time they will crack. It just takes a little drive and for the trials of life to hit them where it hurts. These trials will bring out who they really are.

When we as people learn the who. We can figure out the why and any other questions that may come to mind about the person we are. If you are trying to figure out why you keep going through some of the things continuously with different men. Maybe you have to switch up the type of men you keep picking or change some of the things about yourself. When you are with someone and you have plans of making something real out of the relationship you should have a few things in common with them. There has to be something that will keep you with this person when things get a little rocky.

Believe it or not, love doesn't cover everything in a relationship because even when you love someone if it's over, love will not keep you together. Good looks or a great sense of humor will only take you so far and things of that nature will get old and fade. Even though you would like to date the high school captain of the football team but he doesn't see you sitting next to him in homeroom. You being the nerd and all. Just wait until the ten year class reunion and see if you still feel the same.

The same thing goes for us when we get to the adult stages in our lives. As much as you would like to date the gym rat who lives down the street, you can't. In his eyes you are just another one hundred and eighty pound lady who he doesn't see because he is too superficial to see past you outer appearance. He is just a little shallow and only sees what his eyes allow him to see. You're not the small-framed, petite woman he likes so he will walk right past you like you are not even there. You are not in the best of shape so he will never get the chance to get to know you. The one woman who would really be there for him. It is his loss and you shouldn't let that bother you from going on with your life and being the love someone will truly appreciate.

Even though rejection is something we all don't enjoy dealing with, it happens to us all when we are attempting to find someone. Sometimes it is good to hear the word no or to get rejected because all people are not what they appear to be. That rejection can be the best thing that can happen. Some people are not good for you, so when you get turned down by that hard body, just remember he may just be a shallow-minded, little man that can't find himself. When you are dealing with a man that doesn't even know who he is, it is impossible for him to be able to be there for you completely because he doesn't know how. Getting rejected by this type of man is a good thing because that rejection will save you some time and heartache.

The thing about any aspect of life basically depends on the outlook you have on life it's situations. Some things are more difficult to deal with and some of them are a little bit easier to swallow. Instead of getting down about some of the situations life brings about, you should be thankful you got a chance to get away before things turned bad. You have to find a way to put your pride away in a box and allow some of the things you think you want to just pass you by. Just let go because some things are just not meant to be.

Can you remember your first love and how crazy you were for him and no matter what it was he had done you still covered for him and made up excuses for him. You may not have had anything in common and that is why things didn't work out. As the relationship went on and you started to see he was a two-faced liar, you were finally made strong enough to let go. Although that may have been years ago and you are an adult now, those same boys have grown into men who try the same games. They have gotten a little smarter and more conniving but they still have that same little boy's mentality and motivations. Most men just want one thing nothing else.

If there was a relationship men could have with women without all the headaches and attachments that would be the perfect world for them. That is the world men want but this is a totally different world we live in. Even though your first love was your first he may not be your last and there will be many of trials you will have to go through before you can find Mr. Right and even dealing with him there has to be some work to put in. There is not a man out there who will make you happy 100% of the time. It is just not possible for any of us because mistakes are going to be made. We have to know that no one person is perfect but there is a perfect situation that will present itself when you find the right person that suits you. There is no such thing as a perfect person just someone who is perfect for you.

If you are a talker and you enjoy the occasional midnight talks while laying in bed, the strong silent type may not be the guy for you. It's a little awkward having a conversation by yourself in the dark hours of the night. There has to be something other than sex that ties you to one another. I am one of those people who believe opposites do attract because I have seen relationships like that work. Even though they are different there are things they like that keep them moving in the right direction and in a positive manner. They are so much different in the physical aspect of our relationship they have been given the nicknames Shrek and Fiona.

She is the lovely princess and he the big ole brute. It's not something that bothers him. People sometimes say they don't look like they should be together but they are and care for each other deeply. Although they have been together for a number of years, there is still a lot of growing as a couple they have to do. Love isn't the only thing holding them together, they have grown to be friends. No matter how good love feels to you there isn't anything that will outlast a good friendship inside of your relationship. That's why I say compatibility is so important. You have to be able to find someone who is able to grow with you. The last thing you want to do is to outgrow the person you are in your relationship with.

Long walks in the park while walking the dog, going to the gym, getting a few basketball games in, or just going out to watch a movie. You have to make sure you have someone who doesn't mind a few activities. You can't have a lazy man who wants to sit around the house in his underwear all day. He has to have some get up and go about himself. That's the reason why there are so many couples that have similar jobs, this similarity makes for good conversations and they have learned to bounce ideas off of each other.

Like the pilot and the stewardess. They do well together because they spend so much time together and get a chance to know each other and learn to deal with one and other. Their jobs have similar characteristics. They travel abroad on a regular basis stopping in from city to city and sometimes different cities at the same day. With this type of schedule it makes it hard to have a serious relationship of any kind but it is possible. From time to time, we have to find something or someone that is worth putting in the time for as we would want for someone to do for us. Sometimes you have to make an extra effort depending on your situation. It gets to be hard but it is alright and it will work out as long as you still have some fight in you and you don't get discouraged in your attempts.

You just have to make sure you pick your mates wisely. If you are not the party type, the club hopper may not be the man of your dreams. He is who he is and that won't change until he is ready to change and not any time before that moment. This will keep you from spending so many nights at home alone trying to figure out why he has to go out so much. Its not that he has to go out, it's just he is an out-going person and enjoys the company of others. The problem should come in when you are not invited to the gatherings he attends. If you are not invited there may be something he is trying to hide and it may be a good idea to go to see. If you want to be a home body and watch TV all day there will always be conflicts in your relationship because you are not compatible with each other.

From time to time you have to do something unexpectedly to keep him on his toes. Even though you may have had a long day at work and really don't feel like going out. Sometimes you have to put all of that aside and accompany your man to the engagement to see who his friends are so you can meet them. Maybe you can use the opportunity to spend some quality time with him doing something he likes to do. That will take you a long way especially when it is time to do something you want to do. There will be no questions asked when it's your turn. You do this not just out of curiosity of his actions, you do it to make sure your relationship is peaceful.

When all else fails and you can't seem to find something good in your life, sometimes it's a good idea to just be a little patient and hold out until something good finds you. Occasionally, women start to get frustrated they seem to attract a certain type of man. It may just be a vibe you are giving off that makes them think you are available to them. Even though its hard to hold on when a man isn't being honest with you about who he is and that is why I say stop looking he will find you. You still have to give the world a chance and try to make yourself happy. Because everyone deserves to find some type of peace and happiness in their lives and if the man you are with isn't doing it for you, maybe its time to go ahead and give him his walking papers. It may not end well but I can guarantee you after you get over the breakup the pressure you will release will make you feel so much better.

Remember: Sometimes in life you have to go through a little pain in order to be able to appreciate some of the joyous things life has to offer. It's not a hard concept it's just hard sometimes to keep dealing with the same things over and over again when you don't have to. You are here to make sure some of these days you have spent on this world have been some good ones and you have to do what you can to make that happen. You just have to make sure you are strong enough to deal with the adversities life may put in your way. Also during this time you have to yourself, get to know yourself. It may not be a bad idea to go on a few movie nights alone. Treat yourself on a couple of dinner dates. In this time get to know you so you can be the best you can give to another individual.

SEX

If there was ever a touchy subject when it comes to relationships, this is the one. It is this way because people used to run from the subject because of its nature. But in this era people are more open to the discussion because more people are open to explore their sexuality. The faces that would frown when this subject comes up, will smile now. The mouths that once was closed on the subject are open for to have this talk now. The more people open up you'll find that every individual has their own idea of what sex is and you'll find this because everyone's ideal of sex is different.

The difference comes into play when it is discussed from the mindset of a man and that of a woman. There is a huge difference because when it comes from the mind of a man there is a level of simplicity but when it comes from the mind of a woman there is a level of complexity. This is where the barriers are broken between men and women when it comes to this subject.

When it comes to the mind of a man sex is made simple in his mind. If he desires to have you he will go to the ends of the earth to get you but when he gets you sometimes there is a level of disappointment. It gets to be disappointing because you as a woman may have been expecting something more out of the experience. Not saying the experience wasn't a good one, but women like for a man to put in a little extra effort to show them that they as special and this moment actually meant something.

This presents to be a problem mainly because most men have a lack of an imagination when it comes to sex. There are so many times that you can do the rose petals with the chocolates and the bubble baths before it gets to be boring. Most men don't know that there is a difference between sex and making love. They don't know that sex is the actual act of the physical but there is a mental aspect of making love to a woman. Most men don't know that he can make love to a woman's mind long before he touches her. There is a mental connection that can be made that will last far longer than a sexual one will ever last. This connection can out last the relationship itself but when a couple has this connection in their relationship it will last a lifetime.

Men miss out on the true value of sex because there are so many ways to touch a woman that will set her off in ways they will never know. There's a level of sensuality of women that is ignored because men don't know its there. There are ways that a man can touch a woman that will have her sitting on edge waiting for more. That firm but soft grip that woman like, which helps to set the mood. The look directly in her eyes that lets her know she is the woman he sees. The kiss that is so passionate it lights a fire in you that he can only put out.

When men learn there is an art to having sex and find those ways to satisfy his woman in all the ways that she desires, this is what women want out of their man. This comes with its challenges because even the most knowledgeable men have to learn the woman he is with. Over time he should get to know you so well he knows exactly what to do that helps you to reach your climax every single time while still keeping an open mind for improvement. Maybe adding in some whipped cream, chocolate or even a little candle wax to help keep the spark alive. Sometimes it takes a little more so a few toys may be an avenue that can be taken.

In order for this to happen a man has to get out of his selfish mindset that allows him to think of his pleasures only. To keep that spark alive there has to be a lot of work put in and some creativity to keep everything fun and spontaneous. Being able to have an open mind to sharing each others fantasies is a good way to keep things interesting and can be used to keep you on your toes. Another way to make things a little more engaging is a little role playing

With sex being one of the key elements of a relationship. For men sometimes it is "the key" element in a relationship. Men go well out their way to impress a woman for the final outcome to end in sex. Everything a man does is did for the attention of women. From the way they dress, to the car they drive everything is did to catch the eye of women. But with this superficial mindset he neglects the inner being of a woman. While he is wining and dining you he misses out on the idea of romance because his mind is on the outcome of the night.

He may forget to tell you how beautiful you look. He forgets to hold your hand while you're walking.

Women have a tendency to act as if they are not interested in sex as much as men. When it is all said and done they want it as much, if not more than men. A man has to realize this and make sure nothing is done or said that will spoil the mood. The key point to sex is finding someone who actually pays attention to your body. For most women this is the hard part because most men are naive when it comes to the pleasures of a woman's body. The nature of a woman is made better when a man has found out how to truly satisfy his woman. Please her in ways that she never knew she could be satisfied. For some it is easier said than done but when it is done it is explosive.

When growing up, boys are not taught how to get in touch with their sensitive sides. So by the time they are men words like sensitivity, love or romance are hard for them to define. Being romantic is simple for men who have an active imagination. But for the others this is as hard as flying and airplane. Romance is more than flowers and chocolate on Valentines Day. Its more than a big teddy bear with a random greeting card on her birthday. Most men don't understand the intense texture of romance is what leads to great sex.

The mood of a romantic situation can be brought through some of the simple things that women like. Take for instance cuddling. This is one of the easiest ways for a man to get close to his woman without even trying. A warm embrace topped with an even hotter kiss. This can set the romantic mood for movie night. In the process of the cuddling you actually grow closer as a couple. This quality time isn't just used to set the mood of a night that may end in a night of passionate sex. It also strengthens the bond that you have with one and other.

The romance of it all gets lost in translation sometimes and some men miss out on some of the best sexual experiences they will ever have. The way candles and soft sensual music set the mood of a room. How fruit, hot oils and whipped cream can extend the length of foreplay. Or how mixing alcohol and sex toys can intensify the climax a woman can get. These are a few things about the sexual experience some men miss out on because they are not aware of the wants of the women in their lives.

Some men make the one mistake that no man should. They try to turn the woman they are with into a porno star. Some things in life are better on the television but guys see those things and bring the ideas home. Not saying you can't get anything good from those movies but some of the things they do needs to stay right where they are. These actions will eventually cause disorder in the relationship.

Sex is not meant to be a burden in a relationship but it will happen when sex is looked on the wrong way. Sex is suppose to be the stress reliever not the stress causer. There is nothing wrong with being open with the ideas of your sexual exploits but men have to realize every woman is not made to be a porn star. Some of those things are alright to try but men have to know the caliber of the woman they are with. There are ways to get your woman to open up. There has to be a limit because when it starts to be more painful than pleasurable this may present itself as a problem.

Roll playing is a good ice breaker when it comes to trying new things in the relationship. There is nothing more uncomfortable while having sex than being uncomfortable during sex. When trying something new no one wants to be the one who did something to screw up the mood of the act they are attempting. Mistakes do happen when it is something both of you are new to. The idea is to make sure the memory of this act is one you both will remember and cherish. Not one you will regret.

Spontaneity is one of the key ways to insure you keep your mate on their toes. This one is a real eye-opener when it is done correctly. This level of public affection is one you have to be careful with because you can get in trouble if you get caught. Besides getting caught, this is the one thing that requires an active imagination and a really good sense of timing. These type of sexual impulses are spontaneous and help the couple learn to live in the moment.

This spontaneity also carries over into other areas of your lives. Could you imagine making out in the elevator at your man's office or in the storage closet at yours? Have you ever thought of making out in a movie theater? A dark room with a few people in it while the movie is going on. Would you be open to that? What if your man pulled his car over to the side of the road and proceeded to undress you in the car? Would you play along? What if you are picnicking in a secluded spot in the park? Would you allow the moment to happen? What if he cornered you in the kitchen while you are cooking dinner and he wanted to get a snack before dinner? Would you like to be his snack of chose?

The sexual potential any relationship has is limitless. You just have to be aware of the person and the desires of that person. You get to know your man and he is suppose to get to know you as well. So there will not be any misunderstandings about what the other wants behind closed doors. You learn the limits of how far they are willing to go and you learn physical capabilities of that person. Believe it or not some people are just not physically able to perform every sexual act that is asked of them.

The one thing men have a problem with when it comes to sex is change. The changing of a woman's sexual behavior will cause a man to question it. Even though he may not say a word at first but he soon will. It is good to talk to your mate about theses desires so you will have an open line of communication with one and other. The last thing you want is for your gestures to be taken the wrong way.

Remember: Other than sex being something great to look forward to it is supposed to be something that makes you think of the stars in the midnight sky. Even though you can see them it still doesn't matter if you reach them or not you should still shoot for them every time. The sexual desires of a couple should be a memorable because of the experience shared. With sex being one of the major driving forces of keeping a relationship working, it should be done on a regular basis. Every experience doesn't have to be mind blowing because the occasional quickie is good when time doesn't permit.

LOVE, HAPPINESS, AND PEACE OF MIND

Love is something we all strive for and want in our lives because it feels good especially when it is shared with someone who appreciates it as much as you do. Even though we would like for everyone to feel this way all the time and to be able to share it with everyone in there lives, it doesn't always go the way we feel it should. In a perfect world this would be one of those things you could look forward to but we are imperfect and we live in an imperfect world. This is because everyone doesn't look at love the same way. The definition of it varies with each and every individual.

Before you can be loved, you first have to learn to love yourself. One of the best feelings we can have in this world is when we feel that someone loves us the same way we love them. What feels better than that is when we can learn to love ourselves without having to depend on someone else. Self love should be the first line of offense when it comes to love. As a result you will learn the commendations that come along with love. The way you would treat yourself is the way your better half should treat you. I can't think of one person who would purposely sell themselves short of anything that makes them happy.

Finding love isn't the hard part. Being able to distinguish what the definition of love means to your other half may present a problem. The structure of the relationship can be made easier to deal with when both parties cherish similar traits. Love goes a little deeper than people think. There is a spiritual side of love that helps love to be what it is supposed to be. There is a deepness inside of us which allows us to grow closer to the people we care for. It allows us to open up and experience love the way it is meant.

This spiritual side enables us to look beyond the individuals we are and the flaws we all have so we can learn to open up to reveal to others who we really are. We all have a spirit inside of us and even though the spirit we have is what helps us to be the person we are. We will eventually learn to embrace our spirits and fight our demons. Some people say the spirits of people derives from the spirits of animals. The animals we have inside of us depends on character of our hearts. Our feeling, desires, wants, and needs is what drives us to be the people we are determined to grow into.

The spirit of our being helps us grow a little closer to God and also helps us to be one with self. The better we know self the better we can be for someone else. The animal inside drives us to be better at what we do. This helps us to be better in our lives and better in this world when there seems to be no help and no hope. When love seem to be gone and there is nothing else left there is always hope for the relationship. If we open up to the idea that there will always be someone who will be good to us. This idea will always bring us hope. The spirit inside will always keep us moving in the right direction even when it doesn't feel like we are traveling down the right path. We as individuals deal with things according to its importance to us. From time to time we have to be able to let things go in order to be able to allow ourselves to continue to grow. Let the past stay in the past, deal with the present as it comes, and prepare to deal with future matters with do diligence.

We have to make sure our spirits are in line with one another in order to have a healthy relationship. A lion needs to be in correspondence with a lioness because every pack needs a leader and every leader needs a good fighter in his corner. For everything to stay in working order, this same instinct also keeps us fighting to keep love in our lives. This is what keeps us moving and keeps us looking for love and keeps us trying for love. We all want to find a working relationship that makes us whole and keeps us satisfied in the physical, mental, and the spiritual.

Even though the combination of the three may seem as though it is out of reach, it is obtainable for all of us if we just keep things in order and not settle for less. This order is what allows us to be comfortable enough to accept what is coming our way. It also teaches us patience. Patience to slow down and evaluate to the situations before us. Sometimes things may seem as though they are too heavy for us to bare. During these stressful time are the times we learn to let go. Let go and let our God handle it.

Happiness is not a totally different subject and it is also necessary to building a wonderful relationship. Although the concept of happiness is good to strive for, it takes time to gather the proper components. Happiness comes from within and it derives from a number of different aspects of your life but it comes from the heart first. We all want to be happy in every aspect of our lives. We want a nice job with a good work relationship which is prosperous and promises us a great future. We would like to have a good relationship with our family, friends and every other aspect of our lives. While on this conquest of happiness, there are a few things we will have to bypass.

Most of you knows someone with a negative attitude. A person who doesn't have anything good to say no matter the subject. A person that can't seem to get things right in their lives but has all of the best advise for you. These are the type of people you try to avoid in your conquest for happiness. You avoid them simply because this miserable demeanor can be contagious and could last a lifetime. Everyone knows an old woman who lives with twenty cats and never has a good word to say. What about the old man you try to be nice to? No matter how nice you are or what you try to do for him he still comes across as an old grouch.

If happiness is something you are striving for it can be achieved. When you are truly happy it is something people notice. There is a process that comes along with this feeling. It is not hard to obtain but there is work that has to be put into it. If it is something you want you will do what is necessary to become this way. Happiness is not achieved over night it is something that has to be worked at because it changes a person. It is a process just like any other and a change this deep doesn't just miraculously happen.

It changes people when they have felt it and learn to enjoy the relief it gives. The relief that comes with a peace of mind and a comfort nothing else can bring. When you are happy with who you are and the situation you are in, it helps you to breathe easier and live life more stress free. Happiness is achieved when we are happy with our lives and when mind, body, and soul are one. When all of these are intertwined with one and other, the sun seems to shine a lot brighter, the food we eat seems to be seasoned a lot better, and the smile we share is real and it shines like the morning sun.

With love and happiness there is something else that derives from those two working together the right way. This is called a peace of mind. This peace of mind comes into play when we are satisfied with the person we have grown to be. It gives us the confidence to deal with all the issues life will to bring our way and take them and tackle them head-on according to how they fall. This peace helps us to deal with the issues without getting stressed about them. It helps us to be the rock or the shoulder that some people need in their lives in their times of grief and turmoil. From this our weaknesses are also made stronger. Sometimes it takes people a lifetime to reach this point. The peace of mind to know that no matter what happens in our lives everything will be alright. With this comes an understanding that our Father doesn't put more on us than we can handle.

The pressures of life can get so bad sometimes we don't feel we can make it out the situation we are in. Sometimes this drive us to giving up. These pressures get to be so hectic some people to take their own lives. So don't take it likely. Because once it starts to rain it pours and that there is nothing that we can't accomplish if we keep our Father first and live by his word. Sometimes things can get so bad the only thing that can help to ease the pain is prayer. There is nothing that man can do to make our happiness any better but it is left in the realm of the spirit world.

With living there are issues that come up and will continue to come up as long as we live. Every day brings on different issues and the more level-headed we are the easier those issues are to deal with. He can cheat on you. Even though it may hurt you but you have developed the will to deal with the situation. You can see your way past this and grow to be a better person in order to find someone who is better for you. We will deal with adversity all of our lives and even though these things may crush us, it only breaks us down to allow us to rebuild our structure into the people we are supposed to be.

Sometimes being broken down is a good thing. We have to take a look at who we are and why this is happening to us. There has to be a reason for everything that happens because nothing just up and happens without a purpose. The purpose may be unclear to us in the beginning but who are we to question the reasons why our Father has brought this on us. I think of it on this level, that my Father is always in my corner and the devil is a complete and total lie.

We think it is all in our minds but the truth of the matter is, the devil is always trying to find a way to get in our minds so he can trap our souls. We have to do all we can to avoid the tricks he may pull. At one time the greatest trick the devil ever pulled was to fool the world that he didn't exist. Despite what some may think there are unseen elements at work that are testing our faith. Even though we may be strong and have things in their proper perspective there are things out there that may cause us to backslide. We have to be strong enough to withstand the storm and make the devil regret he ever chose us to pick on.

There will always be adversity in our lives that will present a problem for us but it is up to us to deal with them in the ways we see fit. We all are human and are not immune to making mistakes. The way our parents dealt with the issues of their lives may not be our way in this day and time. It is always good to know what it took for them to get past their problems in order to stop the reoccurring generational mistakes. Even though it may be something they have already gone through. It seems to be difficult for people to take advice. If you would close your mouth and listen sometimes you will see they may have a valid point. We have to realize there is nothing new under the sun. Sometimes a little bit of constructive criticism is what is needed in order to help you see the wrong in your ways. In other times, we may need to get a real harsh dose of reality.

The passive approach isn't good enough to grab your attention. From time to time you need a gut shot to open your eyes and bring you back down to reality. Even though the truth may hurt it is still necessary for us to get to where we are going or where we are trying to go. From time to time we need a real gut shot for the real life situations we face. Sometimes it is good for life to give it to us uncut and raw without any sugar coating in order to get the point across to us. This is mainly for the people who have a problem comprehending it the easy way.

In dealing with relationship issues, the main thing you have to do is remain focused on the one you are in the relationship with. If you focus on yours, you won't have any time to get involved in other people's affairs. You have to make sure you can learn to read them when they are down or are having a problem. You have to make sure you are there for them without being pushy.

Remember: When we can determine what the prioritizes are in our lives we will adapt to the struggles that we are having in a positive way. This will allow us to focus on the important things. Help us to focus on a more peaceful solution to the problems we are having. When we can find our love and happiness, this will allow our peace of mind to grow into something that allows us to enjoy life better. When we enjoy the pleasures of our lives, we become more comfortable and can savor the taste of that delicious main course of life we will be eating. So eat up and I hope that this was a healthy helping of enlightenment that we all can learn something from.

160 | JAWORSKI D. COFFEY

WHAT WOMEN WANT TO KNOW

These are the most frequent questions I have received in my conquest in writing this. I asked a question to get a true idea of what it is women really want to know. So my question to the women was this. "If there was one question you wanted to ask about men and wanted answered honestly by a man, what would the question be?" Through all of the inquiries these are the top questions I received.

Why is it that a man is not satisfied with one good woman?

It is possible for a man to be satisfied with one woman. Men have been doing this since the beginning of time. She has to be more than good. She has to be a great woman. Most men are so self-centered they can't deal with anything for too long without getting bored with it. It is difficult to maintain the concerns of a man who has the attention span of a third grader. The key to a man settling for one woman and spending the rest of his life with her is simple. He has to be willing and ready to lay everything down and give his all to this woman.

What happens in a lot of relationships, is the misconception of there being a relationship. Women get captured in all of the things they do for an ungrateful man who doesn't share the same feelings. A man who is in the relationship for different reasons. A man who is still playing. When a man is in his playing mode he isn't serious about a relationship. Just because you feel you are a good woman doesn't mean you are the good woman for him. He may be looking for qualities of a woman you don't have. Then again you may have come across a man who is not strong enough to handle you.

When men go outside of their relationship they may be searching for something. Instead of taking up whatever the issues are he has with the woman he is with he runs. He runs in search of something he will not find because he has yet to close the doors he has left open. A lot of the time women will confuse what he is looking for with sex but sometimes there is a chance he is looking for something deeper. What you put into the relationship may not be what your man puts into the relationship and its not 50/50. It is supposed to be 100/100. When you are only giving 50% of yourself in a relationship, where is the other 50% going?

Why do men cheat while in a happy committed relationship, or so they say?

The reason why men cheat may be a complex answer or it may be as simple as they do so just because they can. I say this because if a man is in a relationship and an opportunity to cheat comes up and he figures his woman won't find out, the majority of the time he is going to press his luck. What you have to understand ladies is most men don't have the power to say no to the sexual satisfactions that come along with cheating. Something or should I say someone new to have sex with is the most intriguing part about cheating to a man. I have heard men say, "There is nothing like pussy but what's better than pussy is new pussy." Being able to try something new is something men can't seem to pass up. When he does so, it's not something he can say you have done that drove him to cheat. It is not your fault he can't control his urges.

The truth of the matter, if you found out about the women he has slept with and the chances he has taken in doing so, you would be so disappointed in him. The women he has had sex with, most of them, can't hold a glass of water to who you are and will never be able to do the things you have done for him. And let's not mention the time that has been spent in the relationship you will never be able to get back. When a man cheats on you that is a decision he has made and majority of the time it has nothing to do with you.

Why is it so hard for men to commit?

Men have always had commitment issues simply because when men have gotten used to living a certain way, they get comfortable with whom they are and the way things are in their lives. Most men don't want things in their lives to change. What you have to understand about commitment ladies is when he allows you into his life everything is going to change whether he likes it or not. No matter how much you can promise him they won't, we all know that it will. He knows this and letting go of leaving whenever he wants without question is something he isn't ready to let go of. Being able to stay out all times of the night without a worry of having to explain where he has been makes him happy. Being able to have sex with who he wants to when he wants to without fear of getting caught up in an argument because he is cheating is a luxury he is not willing to part with easily.

The main reason men have a problem with commitment is they are just afraid. They are afraid of the responsibility which comes along with having someone they have to answer to. There is a responsibility that comes with a relationship most men have a real problem with. A man has this question that runs through his mind, "Am I ready to be with this one woman and only this one woman for the rest of my life?" Ultimately getting married should be the goal but at this time marriage is the furthest thing on his mind. Outside of being afraid of the idea of committing the mind of a man is a little different and a man thinks the spice of life is variety.

The thought of losing closet space scares him. The idea of having to share his worldly goods scares him. The notion of having to get a bank account that needs two signatures sends chills through him. The idea of a man having to commit to his woman is not a bad one. It is one he has to be willing to do on his own. This means he has chosen to give up his old ways and is ready to explore another chapter of his life.

WHY IS IT SO IMPORTANT FOR A MAN TO HAVE A GOOD RELATIONSHIP WITH HIS MOTHER?

Some women associate their relationship with their man in regards to his mother because if he has a good relationship with his mother, he has already been groomed on how to treat a woman. Most this is correct but this is not a complete science. Most men that have a good relationship with their mother knows how to treat their women but what you women have to realize is you are not his mother. You may be taking care of him like a mother figure like buying him clothes, cars, and maybe even paying his bills and you may even have had his children, but you are not Mom. Men hold their mothers to a higher standard than most things in their lives and no matter how much money you pull out of your purse or the sacrifices you may make for him, you will never reach the level in his mind he has placed his mother on.

There is something good that can come out of his relationship with his mother because there is nothing his mother doesn't know about her son. If there is something you want to know, you can find out from his mother. Ladies what you have to do is pay more attention to your man and get to know him inside-out because this is what pays off in the end. If you want to be held in the same regards as Mom, you have to pay more attention to who he is. His mother had years to groom him into what she wanted him to become. That's why she could read him and could tell when something was wrong because she knew when he was out of his element.

If he wasn't feeling well she could tell what it was just as your mother has done for you. But you have to take in account for the time she has put in with him and that is the reason why he feels as he does about Mom. And outside of everything else you have to realize his mother was one of the biggest influences in his life so he is going to cherish that relationship with all of his heart. What you need to be thankful for is that there was someone in his life that helped to raise him properly for you to be able to enjoy.

WHEN DOES A MAN KNOW HE IS SECURE WITH HIS WOMAN?

When a man is secure with his woman this is the day he is able to make the ultimate commitment to her. This is when he is able to put all of his worldly issues aside and concentrate on just one thing and only one. When a man is able to put his world aside and put his woman first, she should know he holds her in his heart where no other woman is going to ever be able to go. This place he has kept hidden and has never let anyone in.

But marriage isn't what I speak of. Even though it is the ultimate commitment to a woman. It's the point where he opens up to you and reveals every hidden detail about himself he has never told anyone else. He has opened up his heart and soul to you and you have seen a part of him no one has seen since he was a little boy and he was told, "it was not okay for a man to cry."

At this point he has let down the walls of defense. He has allowed you to enter the sanctum of his mind and heart. He is willing to give you everything he has to offer. He will do everything it takes to make you happy. This is when he secure with his woman. He will not hold anything back. He will be able to discuss whatever it is you have on your mind because he wants you to understand him. He has gotten comfortable with how the relationship has grown. He is comfortable with what the both of you have become together. This is what security feels like from a man's perspective.

WHY DO MEN LIKE TO PLAY ON A WOMAN'S EMOTIONS?

Most women deal with the issues in their lives on an emotional scale 99% of the time. Most men are on the rational side of thinkers. Besides the thinking process, a man preys on a woman because men know women are emotional creatures. Women want to be loved and someone to share it with. Women open up and pour out their hearts faster than men. This opens the door for a man to be able to play on your emotions. Men do so because you make it available to them.

It's not that the emotional aspect of a woman is something bad, but it leaves you open and vulnerable to fall for a lot of the problems that you are going to have in your life. Plus it leaves you open for a man to play on them once you show them. Even though men are rational in thinking and everything doesn't have to have any true meaning. Sometimes men wing it and in the process this causes the women in their lives pain. But what women have to know is to a man your emotional status is a weakness to them and they will play on your emotions whenever it is beneficial for them.

If a man is not truly in love with you he will exploit this as a weakness. When a man really loves you he will take you and love you with all your imperfections. He will take you at face value for all you are and all you are worth. A man will try to manipulate you into thinking he is going to be there by your side but once you recognize he is not what he says he is you have to put a stop to it. He can only play with you and your emotions for as long as you allow him to.

DOES A WOMAN'S FEMININITY INFLUENCE AND/ OR AFFECT A MAN'S MASCULINITY?

Yes, yes, yes a woman's femininity does affect a man's masculinity. There used to be a time when it didn't but because in this era most of the women are a lot more aggressive than they used to be which makes it difficult for a number of men to deal with them. The aggressive nature of the modern woman has been known to run off the weaker of the men they will encounter. This aggressiveness, even though it is not the natural nature of the woman, this has changed too. She has more drive and with this ambition this motivates her to be stronger. At this point she is not in a place where she will settle for anything less than she feels she deserves. The femininity a woman possesses is one of the key elements that lets a woman know if the man she is attracted to is a keeper.

If you are an aggressive woman, what you have to remember most men are really intimidated by you and this can be a good and a bad thing.

The good aspect of it is you will run off many of the soft guys who are unworthy of having you. There are some men that will not even approach you because they can sense your strength. If they feel they can't match up with you they will stay as far away from you as possible. It's not so much as him being afraid of you, he just knows the little mind games he likes to play will not work on you because you are focused and will be able to see through them. This is the man that doesn't have any substance about himself. He is the plain glass of water, clear of substance and taste.

But the downside to being aggressive is the same as the up side. There is a level of aggressiveness that will make any man feel uneasy about a woman. There is nothing more uncomfortable to the timid mind of a man than a woman who seems to know exactly what it is she wants. A headstrong women who presents a challenge for most men because most guys would like for things to come to them easy. In dealing with this woman most men have their work cut out for them because this is task a man has to be built for. If he isn't of strong mind and will the pressure of having a strong woman by his side will either build him to be a better man or it will break him and cause him to flee like the rest.

How can a man truly say he loves a woman when he doesn't respect his woman the way he wants her to respect him?

The thing about respect is that it is not given, it is earned. But what makes respect even more controversial is the concept of respect for men and women has different meanings. Respect to women is exactly what it is supposed to be. There is nothing a woman will do that will jeopardize the relationship she has. The time she has put in is so special to her and she will not go outside of her home looking for happiness if there is any hope of salvaging whatever is wrong in her relationship. That's the strength of a woman who knows what she has. She cherishes it and knows the potential the relationship has. So in respect for her man, she will not venture outside of the relationship until the relationship is completely over. That level of respect can't be bought or given, it has to be earned.

But for men, respect means something totally different and it is a little hard to understand. A man feels a lot different because he will go outside of the relationship when things aren't right but he also thinks as long as he is able to pay the bills there should be nothing said about his indiscretions. He feels his respect comes with the financial state of the relationship and the time he spends away from the relationship is not a factor to him either because in his absence his money takes his place.

To be financially stable is one of those factors that make it a lot easier on a relationship but there is more to a relationship than that. Sometimes it doesn't register to some men that if you do go out of your relationship you aren't showing much respect for your woman. When she finds out, it knocks a dent in the armor of the trust she has built in the relationship.

There is nothing like giving the person you say you love a peace of mind.

WHY IS IT THAT MEN CAN ISSUE OUT PROBLEMS TO THEIR WOMEN BUT CAN'T TAKE IT IN RETURN?

What's good for the goose isn't good for the gander. This is a really good topic simply because no matter how strong or tough a man claims to be, he is not strong enough to take the stress of dealing with his woman doing some of the things he would do. It's not that men aren't strong enough it's they can't take it in their hearts. No man wants to hear of his main squeeze has stepped out on him even if he has done the same in the past. It doesn't have to be to the extreme of her cheating on him, it can be him receiving some of the same treatment he has been issuing out to her. When a woman can learn to deal with a man on his level, this presents a problem for the man in the relationship because he can't take being treated like he is the less dominant person of the relationship.

The problem is he gets frustrated when he can't have his way and it gets under his skin when he is getting outsmarted. If it persists, his mind goes into a realm of thinking his woman is testing his manhood and when his manhood is in question he gets on the defensive really hard. The bottom line on the issue is men can't take it. They can't take their women are getting smarter and are growing to be more like them and being able to think like men. Sometimes the issues of the relationship challenges him and he feels like he is less of a man. When the outlook of the relationship changes so does the man.

The outlook of a man's woman learning what buttons it takes to bring him out of his shell and causes him to do something irrational. This is what this learning brings. Even though it's not cool to play these games sometimes it is necessary for women to get their point across to the man in their lives. It helps him to understand the pain his woman has to endure. When the structure of a man is tested this sometimes damages the psyche of this man. This change may not be a pretty sight and it puts stress on him to get things in his life in their proper perspective before things make a turn for the worst.

WHY DO WOMEN HAVE TO ASK THEIR MAN TO GET THINGS DONE EVEN WHEN THE MAN KNOWS IT ALREADY?

This is one of those questions that challenges the responsibility and integrity of the man in the relationship. This is the type of man who wants to be needed in the relationship because with any other man he would do what needs to be done in order to carry his load. The last thing a man wants is to constantly get nagged about pressing issues of the relationship he already knows has to be done. This is one way of stating his dominance in the relationship and it gives him a sense of control over the relationship.

This sense of power allows him to feel he is in charge of the relationship. His power comes in through the power of the dollar and he weighs his worth by that dollar. The financial aspect of the relationship shouldn't determine who the dominant person in the relationship is. A relationship is supposed to be built on an "us" type of mentality. When one of the parties is looking at the relationship in an "I" or a "me" type of fashion this causes problems in the relationship.

There is no "I" in the word team but there are two "I's" in the word relationship. The "I" in ship has to have a number of key participants in order to keep the ship operational. There has to be a captain, the person who calls the shots but also leads to make sure everyone on the ship is doing their jobs to keep the ship on its steady course. It is impossible to have two captains and the captain of the ship has to have earned his position on the ship through hard work and determination. Not from how much treasure he has put into the treasure chest. A relationship is supposed to be a team effort and everyone in the relationship is supposed to do an equal part in order to make sure there are no misunderstandings in the relationship. But when one of the participants in the relationship thinks they are more important than the relationship itself. This causes problems and the biggest problem may be as simple as the man being a procrastinator.

WHY DO MEN PUT OFF THINGS OF IMPORTANCE WHEN THE ONLY THING THEY HAVE TO DO IS TELL THE TRUTH AND TAKE CARE OF SITUATIONS NOW?

When there is a problem, men put things off because most men are natural procrastinators. Men deal with things according to their importance to him. On the small issues men feel it is alright to be this way because it is easier for him to say he will get to it when he gets time. This is a really bad habit to pick up because it is habit forming and rubs off into every aspect of his life. So when it comes to something important this type of attitude is not a good one to have. The natural order of the relationship process is made better when everyone in the relationship does what they are supposed to do.

Most men deal with small matters and big issues the same. Even when the situations are different and some deserve a more in dept approach. His heart may be in the right place but his efforts may show something a little different. Growing up boys are not taught to prioritize as girls are. Girls are raised with more of a caring and responsible nature. Girls are taught to be mothering by playing with their baby dolls, being taught to cook and clean. Boys are taught to be workers and providers but they are not taught the proper skills of prioritizing. Men wing it. Men won't get to the point where most women are in their minds until they become older. Its almost like it is embedded in the DNA of a girl to mature faster than a boy.

This same maturity is what pushes a man to do what is necessary and what is expected of him as a man. This level of maturity varies from each individual. Some guys will get it faster in life, for others it will take a number of years to grasp the concept but there are some who will be so set in their ways they will never get it. We as individuals have to learn our limits. Learn what our physical, mental and emotion limits are before we can trust our hearts to someone else.

ACKNOWLEDGMENTS

First, I would like to give thanks to God who is the head of all our lives no matter the name He has been given. Without Him nothing is possible but through Him the impossible is obtainable. I would like to thank my loving mother Deloris for making the necessary sacrifices in order to influence the man I have become, without her I wouldn't be half of the man I am today.

In the process of living I have lost a few friends but I have gained a few as well, so I would like to thank God for taking those out of my life who weren't meant for me and for those who are still here, I hope you enjoy what I have become. For those who took the time to make yourselves available to help make this dream a reality, I truly and deeply thank you. Uncle Big Ron(RIP), Rodney Cox of Cocki' Photos, Felicia Buckingham of Felicia's Pictures, Cameron "Big Shawty" Elrod(RIP), Andre "Kaliber" Griffin, Chris "Kutta Boi" Powell(RIP); and Tim Bachus of Bachus Entertainment. Also I would like to thank Katrina Griffin for enduring the struggles and heartache that came along in the process of me growing into who I am to become and for that I love you and always will.

To Aiireal, Harmoni, Saria' and Brooklyn Coffey, I would like to say to you all, your daddy loves you and that love for you is why I put together these thoughts and put them on paper. I wanted to be ready for any questions that you may have for me in the future. I know you are a little young now, but for the future I want all of you to know there is nothing you can't ask me or ask of me. If there is anything you want to know and if there is anything I can give, you can have it all. That is why I am here, to make sure all of your needs are met and as your father, I am going to do just that because I want to lead by example and make you proud. But also if God saw fit to call me home before we get around to having these type of conversations, here are your father's thoughts for you all and the world.

CPSIA information can be obtained
at www.ICGtesting.com
Printed in the USA
BVHW072112190722
642490BV00002B/289